e in a review, the reproduction
 form or by any electronic,
w known or hereafter invented,
ying, and recording, and in any
 l system, is forbidden without
ublisher.

 Joe Bannon Sr.
M. Moyer
non
auer

bbart

keting: Kevin King
rs: Michael Hagan (regional),
Maurey Williamson (print)

C.com

ISBN: 1-58261-891-7

© 2004 by Rick Telander

All rights reserved. Except fo
or utilization of this work in
mechanical, or other means,
including xerography, photo
information storage and ret
the written permission of th

Publishers: Peter L. Bannon
Senior managing editor: Sus
Acquisitions editor: Peter L.
Developmental editor: David
Art director: K. Jeffrey Higge
Book design: Dustin J. Hubb
Dust jacket design: Dustin J.
Imaging: Dustin J. Hubbart
Copy editor: Cynthia L. McN
Photo editor: Erin Linden-Le
Vice president of sales and m
Media and promotions mana
 Randy Fouts (national

Printed in the United States

Sports Publishing L.L.C.
804 North Neil Street
Champaign, IL 61820

Phone: 1-877-424-2665
Fax: 217-363-2073
Web site: www.SportsPublishing

"NU's Telander Has Own View of Football" on pages 19-21, by Bill Gleason, originally published in the *Chicago Sun-Times* on Nov. 20, 1970. Reprinted with special permission from the Chicago Sun-Times, Inc. © 2004.

Peoria Journal Star excerpt on page 35, originally published on Oct. 28, 1970. Reprinted with permission of the *Peoria Journal Star*.

"Badger Coach's Protégé Is Back To Haunt Him" on pages 40-41, by Bonnie Ryan, originally published in *The Capital Times* on Oct. 17, 1970. Reprinted with permission from *The Capital Times*.

"NU Clash at Ohio on Campus TV" on pages 44-45, by Roy Damer, originally published in the *Chicago Tribune* on Oct. 29, 1970 and excerpt on page 98, originally published in the *Chicago Tribune* on Nov. 28, 1970. Both reprinted with permission from the *Chicago Tribune*.

(Excerpts from pages 37-39 ...) reprinted courtesy of *Sports Illustrated*: "First Person: The Author Gives Belated Thanks to the Finest Coach He Ever Had" by Rick Telander, August 19, 1985. Copyright © 1985, Time Inc. All rights reserved.

PHOTOS

All interior images are from the author's collection, with the exception of:
Page 65: United Press International
Pages 70, 78: Courtesy of Northwestern Athletics
Page 85: Reprinted with permission by the *Peoria Times-Observer*
Page 87: Photo by Mary Anne Peeler
Page 103: Courtesy of Rich Clarkson and Associates
Page 106: Courtesy of the Kansas City Chiefs
Page 125: Courtesy of the *S.F. Examiner*

Every reasonable attempt has been made to determine ownership of copyright. Please notify the publisher of any erroneous credits or omissions, and corrections will be made in future printings.

To Jeje and Sweetie, my parents

Contents

Warmups 1

Kickoff 10

First Quarter 24

Second Quarter 46

Halftime 58

Third Quarter 76

Fourth Quarter 100

Overtime 116

"Football is like a rose."

—Carlos Alvarez,
University of Florida All-America wide receiver, 1970.

Warmups

Football is the oddest, meanest, sweetest game. It is a conflict at its root and at its surface. It pulls a sane person in two directions—anger and joy. At times players literally fight one another, and at times they are bound together in a dance. Baseball, it has been said, is America's pastime; football its passion.

Give me passion.

My life has been full of football. I didn't plan it. I didn't anticipate it. I am middle-aged now, but thoughts of the game are never more than an eyeblink away. There is that game against Peoria Bergan High School. I am the 17-year-old quarterback for Richwoods High School, and we are a better team than Bergan. Everyone knows this. My ex-girlfriend who goes to Bergan knows this. Why do I turn the wrong way on the goal-line bootleg—which I have called—and get tackled for a safety?

The bird that lands on my Northwestern teammate and preseason All-America candidate John Voorhees's hand, in the middle of a miserable, two-a-day, August lecture from frothing defensive coach Pat Naughton, like a sign, like a miracle. Why?

When I wanted to quit college ball, give up my scholarship, when the world of war and protest made my life seem so small and irrational and I thought my head would explode from the turmoil within, my dad, who had never played football, the former World War II bomber pilot who worked and raised a family the way men of his generation did, was there saying to me: I understand, but you should think about this, because time goes by and you have only this one chance, and then it is gone.

He was right. And I thank you, Dad.

And I thank you too, Mom. You didn't want me playing this game. You asked me not to, and you suffered and covered your eyes when I did. Mothers protect. They don't risk. I learned a lesson because of that: Football is a man's game. All that is flawed and uncontrollable and beautiful about men is there in it.

I have been a professional sportswriter now for over 30 years, and what I have seen is that America is fascinated by football, consumed by football. America worships football. But it doesn't praise football. It is as though we are embarrassed by our passion.

There are poems to baseball. There are enough golf novels to rebuild a forest. There are big, happy movies about horseracing and basketball, soccer and surfing, bike riding, and did I mention baseball? But football stands in the corner, shuffling its feet. No one pats football on the back, says thank you for being who you are.

I have been seeking truth all my life, even when unaware of that and when doing incredibly stupid things, and I have failed miserably in my haphazard search. The reading, the listening, the religion classes, the philosophy studies, the anger, the cynicism, the debating, the propped-up hopes, the lazy cop-outs, the ceaseless pondering that leads in a circle back to where it began—the understanding that all things end—nothing has gotten me to where I want to be. And yet the game is always there.

You read about football in two ways. Football is about heroes and champions. Football is about nastiness and pain. I have written both. Both are half wrong. Football is a paradox. It is this and that, one thing and the other, many things at the same time. What I want to say in this book is what I think the truth about football is.

Maybe you will get something like that from my old diary or my talks with my high school coach. Maybe you'll get a kick out of the old newspaper stories I reprinted. Maybe you will see it in my random thoughts, dropped in like bookmarks. Maybe I cannot express it at all, having bumped up against my limits as a writer.

But what I want to say is that football is like a rose, the way Florida wide receiver Carlos Alvarez put it so well years ago. I want to say that football has cut me and hurt me and confused me and adorned me and sweetened the air I breathe. I want to say that I now know it is something special, and that I love it.

Kansas City Chiefs Football Club
5605 East 63rd Trafficway
Kansas City, Missouri 64130
Henry "Hank" Stram
Head Coach

June 24, 1971

Rick Telander
6004 Sherwood
Peoria, Illinois 61614

Dear Rick:

This letter will serve as your official notification to report to our training camp sight by Tuesday noon, July 20, at William Jewel College, Liberty, Missouri, for the 1971 season.

All players, rookies and veterans, must report on this date, July 20, by noon at the dining hall in the Union Building. The first meal will be served at that time. Tuesday afternoon will be devoted to physicals, dentals, and checking out equipment. Wednesday, July 21, at 9 o'clock will be picture morning. Meetings will occupy your extra time Wednesday and our first practice session will get under way at 9 o'clock

Thursday morning, July 22. I cannot emphasize too strongly the importance of being here on time. Do not ask to report late because only those in the All-Star Game in Chicago and men in the service will be excused. A fine of $500 will be imposed on anybody arriving late.

The Kansas City Chiefs will furnish shoes and all necessary equipment, but you must furnish your own practice shoes. All players must report cleanly shaven—no mustaches, goatees, or over-exaggerated sideburns will be permissible in training camp or during the regular season. Pets and firearms are also not permissible.

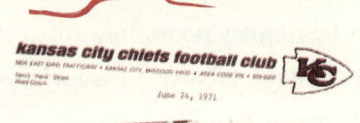

6 Rick Telander

You have seen my basement in horror movies. It's the basement with the narrow staircase, the cobwebs dangling from rough-hewn wooden beams, the unpainted brick walls, and the bare lightbulbs that can be lit only by tugging on the various-lengthed strings that dangle from the unfinished ceiling.

I try to avoid going down to the basement at night. Funniest thing, but I am probably more afraid of the dark now than I was as a kid. I recall the life-altering moment well. It was 1982. I was in Midland, Texas, writing a piece for *Sports Illustrated* about junior college basketball phenom Spud Webb. I spent time with Spud on campus, measured the wee guy's vertical—48 inches—and then went back to my hotel, ate dinner, and turned on the tube. I started watching *Halloween II*, and before I knew it, Michael Myers had crept out of so many places and killed so many people, including boiling one victim in the hot tub, that I turned off the TV, turned on the lights, bolted and chained the door and did not sleep that night. When the sun came up, I dozed off.

At any rate, I went down to my basement in broad daylight a few months ago and attempted to find something in the old trunks that line the shelves. I believe it was a photograph I was searching for. But I don't recall. I wiped away the dust and, ahem, mouse evidence on many surfaces, moved old train sets and holiday decorations and roller blades and rummaged through several boxes in the dimly lit and cluttered area. Then I lifted the lid off a lopsided, cardboard trunk. Clippings. Mementos packed away by somebody years ago. Old photos. Me, age 10 months, in a crib with my cousin, Tory, age 14 months. My sisters. My folks. Our old house in Peoria. A broken picture frame. Me, growing older. Playing games. Sports snapshots. Yellowed newspapers. Envelopes. And then: a tiny notebook.

Something spun inside me. "K.C. Chiefs Diary," it said. My God, I wrote this. How many years had it been since I had seen it? Since I thought of it? What did it say?

I unfolded a chair and sat down. There in the basement I started reading.

Kickoff

Monday, July 19

I got to the dorm and dumped my stuff. Here I am.

Most of the rookies mill about, and since it's a nice day a lot of the guys hang out on the steps or the grass in front. You can tell the rookies, since we're generally the smaller, younger, more timid-looking guys.

We came on buses or in cabs, and we watch as several late-model Grand Prix and Cadillacs rumble into the parking lot and disgorge famous, rich-looking veterans. They saunter past, ignoring our presence or else giving the whole group a blanket hello.

"How's it going, men?" All-Pro linebacker Bobby Bell says.

"Fine. Just fine," we chant as he disappears into the building.

"How'd you like to meet him in a dark alley?" somebody says.

We all snort and shake our heads. More veterans arrive.

There are long pauses in our conversation.

"You know gas only costs 21 cents a gallon here?" somebody says.

"Amazing," somebody replies.

Another pause.

"Well, so long."

"Yeah, I'm going to watch TV."

People drift off, some to sleep, some to read, some to eat at the local Dairy Queen.

I'm hungry, so I go off to eat.

I had never played quarterback in tackle football. In high school I played wide receiver, tight end, safety, and for a brief time defensive end from my freshman year until the end of my junior year. And then, in a twist that still amazes me, I was abruptly the senior starting quarterback for Richwoods High School.

Quarterback. Field general. The guy.

It changed my life. I had seen the peak.

My coach, Tom Peeler, tapped me. We worked through that summer before my senior season, him personally, hands on, teaching me everything I didn't know. We started with standing behind center. This is how you do it. Bend your knees. Not too much. I learned how to "lap" the ball before handing off. I never before had heard the term. There's the 2,4,6,8, and zero holes. Over yonder are 1,3,5,7,9. Peeler was a small-town southern Illinois native, and he occasionally said things like yonder. This is your first step, this is your second. Fingers go on the laces like so. This is how you survey your kingdom when both lines are down and the world has calmed to a super-slow-motion sequence in a silent movie.

I became the quarterback. I led our team to a homecoming win, took five stitches in my chin, and squired to the homecoming dance the girl who most people believed to be the prettiest in our school. Wow.

Why was I made into the quarterback?

It's a curious thing, but I never thought to ask.

From the "Quarterback Manual" given to me by my high school coach Tom Peeler at the start of my training:

"The "Wing T" quarterback has a unique part in the successful operation of this offense. His greatest contribution will come through the medium of calling a smart game rather than solely by his physical efforts. A quarterback can have all the speed, ruggedness, passing ability, and faking finesse, yet never rise above mediocrity if he isn't thinking every minute of the game. His physical abilities may be dissipated through inopportune use, yet by calling a smart game and hitting the enemy at his weak point, the quarterback can help just fair personnel to do a better than average job. It goes without saying that a "football-wise" quarterback, possessed of tremendous physical ability will be of great value to his team. But it should be understood that mental ability and average physical capabilities will make a better quarterback than one with tremendous physical ability and a below-average football mind."

Craig Williams was an undersized offensive guard for Richwoods High, a hard-working kid who gave everything he had. He was the kind of blocker a quarterback loved. I loved him. As you stand back there like the big cheese, dancing around, patting the ball, stepping up, back, looking through the kaleidoscope of jerseys and grunting, snot-faced sub-humans swarming your way, you appreciate a guard knocking the living crap out of a defender now and then.

But Williams was slow. Foot speed, they call it now. He didn't have any. Coach Peeler, tall, graying-haired, always with a green baseball cap on his head and a whistle around his neck, had a way of standing during practices that showed extreme attentiveness combined with a certain reserved bemusement. We were running a power sweep in practice, and Williams just wasn't getting there in time. Again and again. Everything was fouled up. We offensive players stopped after one more attempt and stood panting, looking at our coach for direction. Peeler nodded. His arms were folded on his chest. It was clear he had analyzed the situation and knew the problem.

"Son," he said to Williams in his slow, easy voice, "you're slow as smoke comin' off manure."

Kansas City Chiefs Football Club
5606 East 63rd Trafficway
Kansas City, Missouri 64130

April 14, 1971
Rick Telander
1847 Asbury
Evanston, Illinois

Dear Rick:

Enclosed please find your bonus check for $3,000.00, and your copies of the addendum and also the contract as per our agreement.

Good luck and best wishes.

Kindest regards,
"Hank"
Henry Stram,
Head Coach

kansas city chiefs football club
5605 EAST 63RD TRAFFICWAY • KANSAS CITY, MISSOURI 64130 • AREA CODE 816 • 924-9300

April 14, 1971

HENRY "HANK" STRAM
HEAD COACH

Rick Telander
1847 Asbury
Evanston, Illinois

Dear Rick:

Enclosed please find your bonus check for $3,000.00, and your copies of the addendum and also the contract as per our agreement.

Good luck and best wishes.

Kindest regards,

Hank

Henry Stram,
Head Coach

HS:pc

Enclosures

Oh, how I remember that bonus check! More money than I had made in my life. I negotiated with Stram at our first mini-camp, and he agreed to give me $500 more than his original bonus offer of $2,500. "But I'll have to take a thousand dollars off your annual contract," he added sternly.

Absolutely, I said, nodding. I understand. Makes sense. My contract, should I make the team, thus became $15,000 instead of $16,000.

When the big yellow bonus check with red lettering came in the mail that spring of my senior year, I taped it to the mirror above the fireplace in the living room of the massive and stunningly decrepit three-story house I rented along with 11 other Northwestern students. I left the check there for days. It was a shrine to kneel before, a trophy from the hunt, a work of art.

Who could steal it? Who could cash it? Nobody.

It was too huge.

**The *Chicago Sun-Times*
"NU's Telander Has Own View of Football"
By Bill Gleason**

November 20, 1970

Nobody is more dazzled than I by the athletic skills of the hockey-playing bears in the Moscow Circus on Ice, but I have to rank them No. 2 behind the best act in these parts. The top spot belongs to the four acrobats who play pass defense for Northwestern's football team.

If there should be ice on the rug at East Lansing, Michigan, Saturday afternoon, the Northwestern quartet will come skating out for its season-ender against Michigan State. The other night at the Amphitheatre, when the ice-making machine failed to function, the Moscow bears caucused and decided the show would go on without them.

No pass defense foursome has been given so much ink around here since Roosevelt Taylor and Richie Pettitbon were playing between Bennie McRae and Davie Whitsell.

Alex Agase, Northwestern's headman, has a fine foursome, reading from left to right: cornerback Jack Dustin, strong safety Mike Coughlin, free safety Eric Hutchinson, and cornerback Rick Telander. All are juniors except Telander, who is their unacknowledged leader.

"I try to talk to them once in a while," said Telander, who takes himself and his football about as seriously as Alex Karras does. "But nobody listens to me. I tell them I get all these interviews this season because they're too ignorant to represent Northwestern properly, but I've also told them that when I'm gone next year they should reminisce in their interviews about how great I was."

Part of a good group

Telander is ribbing himself—that's my assumption, at least—but the unit is truly great. This week Northwestern moved to second in the nation for forward pass defense, just behind Toledo, which finishes with Colorado State.

Hutchinson has intercepted six passes, Dustin four, and Telander three. When Northwestern has the ball this year there is plenty of excitement, and the entertainment doesn't stop when Telander leads his merry group into the combat. The leader is equally entertaining off the field as these quotes so subtly hint:

"I was a quarterback at Richwoods High School in my senior year, but my receivers used to throw the ball back to me harder than I had thrown it to them. They even threw better spirals. Honest, we had one end who could really throw a beautiful spiral. So I'd run 15 times a game.

"I played high school basketball, too. I used to jump around a lot, but I didn't have much of a shot. Basketball was nice, especially after football. It was nice to go inside and be warm.

"Did I ever think about playing professional football? I never thought I'd be able to play high school football. Everybody was always telling me I was too skinny, and I was.

"What I think about every once in a while is what if nobody had invented a pointed ball, a ball pointed on both ends? What would football be as a sport? There wouldn't be any football."

So long ago. But I remember columnist Gleason well. We sat in an empty coach's room at Anderson Hall next to the practice fields, and I regaled him—or so it seemed to a concerned, overflowing 21-year-old--with postadolescent intelligence and wit. In 15 years our paths would cross again when Gleason, his red hair a brilliant white by then, would ask me to be one of the original members of *The Sportswriters on TV* show.

What he didn't realize at the time of our earlier interview was that he said something incredibly meaningful to me. At one point, as I babbled on—dear God, could I really have spoken words as moronic as, "It was nice to go inside and be warm"?, he stopped his note-taking and looked at me through his large, dark-framed glasses.

"You should be a writer," the legendary Chicago columnist said. He may have chomped harder on his cigar at that point. He may have winked. I remember I thanked him for his words. But I didn't let on. Inside I was aflame.

I had always wanted to be a writer.

But no one had ever told me I should be.

I wondered about so much. I got older, and I wondered more.

Why did Tom Peeler make me his quarterback?

THINGS LEARNED FROM FOOTBALL: Your past achievements are less relevant than spoons in a fork drawer.

First Quarter

Tuesday, July 20

Everybody's here. They came in from all over. It's uncommonly cool and dry for this area, a fact that is slightly ironic since we don't start practice until tomorrow afternoon when a new low-pressure system is due.

At the meeting we introduced ourselves and said our college name. It made sense for the rookies since we're straight from school, but to hear Len Dawson say, "Purdue University" was too much.

I stand on the sidelines at this lumpy field on a cold October night, looking at the little football players moving about like toy men on a vibrating table. I have my doubts. My nine-year-old son, Zack, is out there with the other third-graders. Many are from his school, our neighborhood. Some are from the Catholic school a couple miles away, or the next town.

This is tackle football for nine-year-olds. Those stalk-like necks and wandering minds were not designed to be encased in unbreakable headgear. And the knees and fingers and spines? These are just little kids who would be better off, it seems to me, running about in somebody's back yard, playing tag, climbing trees, rolling down hills.

One of my main pleasures in life is putting Zack to bed, reading to him, and checking on him through the night. Not long ago I came in from my office after midnight and opened his door. I studied his unlined features in the soft light. The house was silent. Judy and the three girls were long asleep.

I leaned over and rearranged his dinosaur sheets, pulled up his blanket, straightened his dinosaur pillow. What was underneath? An envelope. It was unsealed, and I looked inside. A folded note. I went out into the hall where my old eyes could read.

Dear, Toothfairy
I lossed my tooth but I accedentily swallowed it. I am very sorry I didn't have a tooth for you.

Dear Toothfairy

I lossed my tooth but I accedentily swallowed it. I am very sorry. I didn't have a tooth for you

How do I square that with this? My son, polite to a fantasy.

But Zack had been adamant about tackle football. If I, as a dad who had played the game, had told him, No, you can't play. It's too dangerous!—well, I couldn't.

Now a running back is moving. He takes the handoff from the uncertain quarterback, sees the blockers on the line milling about and runs toward the sideline. Almost every play in this league turns into a sweep. Passes are rare, completions far rarer. Sweeps are continuous.

The boy tries to cut upfield, and there is a stuttering collision and a pileup. Zack, the linebacker, is in the middle of it all, as little bodies stack up, others falling slowly the way late bowling pins do.

Players stand up. Zack rises. His orange jersey says No. 52. He watched Ray Lewis tackle on TV and he liked that, and during sign-ups he asked for Lewis's number. Next year he will ask for No. 54, Brian Urlacher's number. Zack's team is called the Suns, and players have a small white sun on each sleeve. The sun looks like a happy face.

At least this league is safe, I say to myself. The field is small, and players are set apart by three weight classes, so that bigger guys are on the line at first and smaller ones in the offensive and defensive backfields, and middle-sized ones play special teams. Periodically the groups rotate so that the smaller boys are on the line, the bigger ones become special-teamers, etc. Zack is one of the bigger guys, even though he is so skinny his pants fall down. Genetics.

I see him walk toward the ref as the teams return to their huddles. He has something in his closed fist. He gets the ref's attention, appears to ask him something, then hands him whatever he has in his palm. He jogs back to his team.

I saunter casually around to the other side of the field, and during a break I ask the ref what the boy, No. 52 in orange, gave him.

"A tooth," says the ref. "His."

Tom Peeler. I had two wonderful coaches in my life. He was one. The other was my defensive backfield coach my junior year in college, Bob Zeman. Ag was a good coach, but he was an overseer, not my personal mentor. And we had our difficulties.

I find myself thinking about Peeler and Zeman more and more.

I wonder if they are alive.

I wonder where they are.

Like a Rose 29

June 26, 1971

Media Guide
11th Annual Coaches All-America Game
Jones Stadium, Texas Tech University
Lubbock, Texas

*Assistant Coach, East Team, Alex Agase Northwestern football coach, Alex Agase, whose athletic career has been replete with honors, achieved the greatest yet in 1970, when the Football Writers of America named him National Coach of the Year.

This was one of the rare occasions when the award went to a coach for achievements other than producing a national or conference champion. In producing a Big Ten title contender and one of the surprise teams of the country, Agase proved that Northwestern, the Big Ten's smallest school, could challenge for league and national honors. He took a team that had been picked to go nowhere and led it to second place with a 6-1 record, just one game behind undefeated Ohio State.

The 48-year-old Agase was an All-America guard twice at Illinois during a career interrupted by World War II. He achieved the same honor while a marine trainee at Purdue. As a marine he earned the Bronze Star and Purple Heart in action on Okinawa. He then returned to lead Illinois to its legendary 45-14 rout of UCLA in the 1947 Rose Bowl game.

Like a Rose 31

Ag, as we knew him, was short, square-bodied, with a head like a granite tombstone. I knew about granite tombstones from my high school summers spent working at the Peoria Cemetery, where my buddy Bill Blair and I had the duty of traveling about the vast, old graveyard in a jeep, with picks and shovels, and re-standing headstones that had been erected as far back as the late 1700s and had tipped over with time. I studied Ag as he moved between drills and decided he was put together like an ancient stone totem from a South Pacific island.

He was gruff, focused, without subtlety, stubborn, simple, honest, kind—to a point; this was football, you know—and fair, and if there wasn't an unlit cigar planted in the corner of his mouth, as fidgety as a baby without a pacifier. Since he couldn't smoke or even chew a cigar during games, he would bend down and grab the next best thing—sideline grass. Before kickoff the growing cud in his lip would have turned the corners of his mouth kelly green. When we Wildcats played our first game on artificial turf, I remember watching poor Ag crouched over, reflexively tugging at chunks of plastic fiber that wouldn't give way. Oh, he suffered on artificial turf.

Coach Agase was the war hero. And I was the dubious and confused antiwar skeptic. Ag and I circled each other at times, each cautious about the other. Vietnam loomed for all of us players. If our student deferments gave out or we graduated, and we passed our draft board physicals, we were gone. Ag had played in the Good War. And done it right. Like my dad. But what was the Vietnam War? Who was the opponent? What was the offense? Where was the goal line? No, it was worse than that. What was the game?

In spring practice of my freshman year, I was struggling as a wide receiver. My mind drifted. Balls sailed through my hands.

"Jesus, Telander, catching the ball is easy if you concentrate," said Ag. He lumbered over and stood beside me. "*I* can catch the ball."

He told Dana Woodring, a varsity quarterback with a rifle arm, to stand 15 yards away from him and fire the ball at him. Reluctantly, at first, Woodring did. Thunk. The ball stuck in Ag's stubby, middle-aged, ex-lineman's fingers. Thunk. Thunk. Again and again. The coach moved five yards closer. "Throw it!" demanded Ag. Woodring heated up. He threw sizzlers. He threw peas. Ag caught every one of the fireballs. His gooey cigar barely moved. I was astounded. And impressed.

"See?" said Ag.

I nodded. He left, and I thought about it all. I concentrated. Passes still went through my hands. I worried about the war, about classes and deep books and elusive lectures and the hints of solace and even greater questions within, about the certitude of football and the shadow of the unknown. It seemed to me that a war should be far clearer than a game. And Vietnam was nothing but murk, a nightmare of uncertainty. In football you could be the aggressor, run the patterns, catch the ball. Or you could play defense and react. My high school quarterbacking days were gone. Wide receiving was dim. But I could make this game clear as glass. It could be my anti-Vietnam. By December I knew I wanted to react. I would tackle and try to catch the bad balls, the overthrows and tips, the mistakes. There would be no doubt for me.

I became a defensive back.

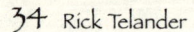

PEORIA JOURNAL STAR October 28, 1970

The latest batch of NCAA statistics showed Northwestern sixth in the land in pass defense, and aside from Ivy Leaguer Dartmouth, the other four were from the second echelon of major college football—San Diego State, Bowling Green, Dayton and Rutgers.

And the Wildcats have done their amazing pass coverage against some of the nation's best...

"They have the best pass defense I've seen all year," Notre Dame quarterback Joe Theismann praised a few days ago. "They laid back eight yards, so I thought I could hit short. But when I threw they were there. Then I threw long and they were there, too."

Telander & Co. completely smothered Mike Wells of Illinois and Neil Graf of Wisconsin. Wells managed just 10 yards through the air and Graf, who faced the Wildcats as the Big Ten's passing leader, completed just three of 15 for 32 yards.

Joe Theismann. I remember him well. He was the hyperactive All-American-to-be whom Notre Dame PR man Roger Valdiserri had once said seemed to have his finger stuck in an electric socket.

In my very first game as a cornerback, as a junior in our opener in South Bend, under the fearsome glare of Touchdown Jesus and the shrieking Domer faithful, Joe Theismann dropped back to throw the first pass of the season.

I stepped in front of the wide receiver, All American Tom Gatewood, in the right flat and the ball hit me in the chest. It felt like a dream. I was out of my body, watching myself run forward and get tackled by some monstrous offensive linemen. One pass. One interception.

It couldn't be this simple, could it?

CHICAGO TODAY January 30, 1971

PHILADELPHIA—The National Football League draft, a big newsmaker yesterday, droned into its second and final day this morning, picking up in the eighth round with only long shots remaining.

Of course, long shots sometimes come through. ...But they're the exceptions rather than the rules...

Of Chicago area interest was the addition of three more Northwestern players to the list, joining running back Mike Adamle, who was plucked by Kansas City in the fifth round yesterday.

Joining him today were defensive back Rick Telander, to Kansas City in the eighth round...

There were many things my Northwestern secondary coach Bob Zeman taught me in that first year that I moved to cornerback from wide receiver. But prime among them were calm, acceptance, and the lasting worth of decency. In April of my sophomore year we began spring practice, and due to graduation and good fortune, I was penciled in as the starting right cornerback, even though I had never played a down at that position.

Zeman was new to the coaching staff, having only recently finished his own playing days as a defensive back for the San Diego Chargers and Denver Broncos. In the secondary's first meeting Zeman diagrammed a play on the blackboard. He looked at me and said, "Dave, what do you do here?"

My name is Rick. I have a distant cousin named Dave, but he's many years younger than I, and he wasn't born yet. But I couldn't correct my new coach. It would have been arrogant and perhaps career-ending for my first words to him to be, "My name's not Dave." My hold on that first-team spot was the definition of tenuous. I could see myself bouncing down the depth chart for appearing to be a cocky ass. So I answered the question and said nothing about my name.

As spring practice progressed, Zeman continued to call me Dave. Good plays, bad plays. Dave it was. Where would this end? The longer it went on, the more embarrassed I felt—for myself and for him. I didn't know how to get out of the mess. Each time he called me Dave, I flinched.

Then one day in a meeting he looked at me and said, "Your name's not Dave."

I looked up to see what he would do. If a tough guy thought I had been trying to make him look foolish, he would have thrown me out of the meeting. A real tough guy might have run me till I puked.

What Zeman did was smile. And then he blushed. It was a nice thing to do.

Zeman wasn't a pansy. He'd been the co-captain of Wisconsin's 1959 Big Ten championship team. But he had a fundamental courtesy and calm that was like a balm for me, the skittish, ever-worrying DB. All of us in the secondary worshipped him. He taught technique and preparedness. But he taught something else. He taught that bad things will happen. They would happen naturally, he let us know, in the natural order of things, as part of life, as a fundamental axiom of this game we played. But you couldn't let them get you down.

Receivers will catch passes, he said. He'd shrug, grin. "That's OK. Everybody makes completions. It's no big deal."

That simple blessing made me soar. It was like the inverse of the old cliché: Life's a bitch, then you die. Enjoy the ride while it's here, is what Zeman was saying. Don't sweat the little things. Don't sweat the inevitable. Come back. Forget. Move forward. Get on. His words freed me from fear and let me play.

The next year he took the defensive backfield job with his alma mater, Wisconsin. And I missed him a lot. But he had prepared me.

Like a Rose 39

October 17, 1970

THE CAPITAL TIMES, Madison, Wis.
Badger Coach's Protégé Is Back
to Haunt Him
by Bonnie Ryan

When he was a junior in Richwoods High School in Peoria, Ill., he thought that Northwestern University was in the state of Indiana.

Now, he not only knows that Northwestern is in Evanston, Ill., but he also is helping put Northwestern on the map.

He is Rick Telander who will start this afternoon at right cornerback on the Wildcats defensive unit.

Rick is a senior. Not only is he talented on the football field, but also in the classroom. He was named to the first-team All-Big Ten Academic team last year.

Telander also has a close connection with Wisconsin.

The gentleman responsible for Rick being a defensive back is Bob Zeman, Wisconsin's defensive backfield coach.

But Zeman was Northwestern defensive coach when it happened.

Rick started out as a split end. He caught two passes there as a sophomore. But he still didn't play much.

Then last year Zeman was looking for talent for his defensive unit. He looked to the offense and spotted Telander, who wasn't being used sufficiently.

"I could use him," Zeman told head coach Alex Agase.

"He turned out to be a real surprise," said Zeman. "He is quick. He plays one on one well. He reads receivers' moves. He has the ability to hit."

He was the best back coached by Zeman in his two years at Northwestern.

Telander's quickness is revealed in that he has been clocked at 4.6 for the 40-yard dash.

The former end will be busy this afternoon watching Badger ends. And former Northwestern coach Bob Zeman is hoping that he will be back at end again.

And that Rick Telander would go back to his high school days when he thought Northwestern University was in Indiana.

Wednesday, July 21

A person 6'2" is taller than most people in a crowd, right?

And if you're about 195 pounds then you're also bigger than most people—isn't this a simple mathematical fact?

Then how come when I, who am the above, stand in the locker room or in the shower or in line anywhere with all the other Kansas City Chiefs I feel like an undernourished dwarf?

Of course, you know why, very good. It's because I'm surrounded by giants. For example: Buck Buchanan—6'7", 275 lbs.; Morris Stroud—6'10", 250 lbs.; Aaron Brown—6'6", 270 lbs. (Buck Buchanan said to him the other day: "Damn, Aaron! You got the legs of a man eight-foot-three and five hundred pounds. Shee-it!" And it's true. Although Brown is already built on a massive scale, his head, arms, and shoulders are only normally huge. His legs are like, well, like tree trunks.); Jim Tyrer—6'6", 270 lbs. Hell, the list is endless.

Today before our first warm-up lap they divided us into six groups according to our positions. The tackles and ends ran in front of the defensive backs. Now, there is a very definite philosophy of men who work hard and know their own ability and also know what they need to do to succeed. They firmly believe that you push yourself when it is important, but not when the goal is unequal to the punishment. Case in point: You push yourself in scrimmages, football technique drills, and games. You do not push yourself in half-speed warm-up exercises.

Mr. Buchanan was very unsubtle in delivering the point of this philosophy. Staring back at we measly, anemic-looking defensive backs, he said with a seriously ominous voice, "Don't you fellows get too antsy back there. The man said half-speed, you hear! Don't be runnin' on my tail or I'll have to whup some ass."

I dare say he could have whupped some ass, too. Probably the whole bunch of our asses at once. So we kept our distance.

October 29, 1970

CHICAGO TRIBUNE
NU Clash at Ohio on Campus TV
by Roy Damer

Northwestern University students never have been known to go wild over their football teams, seemingly regarding them as something that exists in Dyche Stadium on about five Saturday afternoons in autumn.

But a 3-0 record in the Big Ten has changed that blasé attitude and a refreshing "demonstration" took place on the Evanston campus this week.

It all wound up with the announcement that the Northwestern-Ohio State game would be shown on closed-circuit television in McGaw Hall Saturday. The doors will open at 11:30 a.m. for the 12:30 p.m. kickoff, and all seats will be $2 with none reserved.

The whole thing was started by two students who wanted to see this battle of unbeaten teams in conference action. The *Northwestern Daily*, the school newspaper, got behind it and the ball was rolling....

Henry Higginbottom, a graduate student, and George Coakley, a senior, launched the project.

The $2 fee is nominal for such an attraction, but Higginbottom explained: "We just wanted to have the game on campus and are interested in a good crowd.... You remember the movie, *Goodbye Columbus*? Well, in advertising the game on campus we're going to use the theme, 'Goodbye Columbus, Hello Rose Bowl.'"

THINGS LEARNED FROM FOOTBALL:
You can have the shit knocked out of you in a game. It happened to my high school fullback, Paul Avery, and my quarterback at Northwestern, Maurie Daigneau. Both needed fresh pants.

Second Quarter

November 5, 1970

CHICAGO DAILY NEWS
N.U. Gears For Gopher Air Attack

Northwestern's alert secondary defense, which has held seven opponents to a pass completion average of 32 percent to rank among the nation's leaders, is gearing for another stiff test Saturday against Minnesota quarterback Craig Curry, who leads the Big Ten in completions and total yards.

The Wildcats' fine pass defense achievement has been compiled against some of the nation's best passers, including Notre Dame's Joe Theismann, UCLA's Dennis Dummit, SMU's Chuck Hixon and Ohio State's Rex Kern.

Opposing passers have been limited to 45 completions in 139 attempts and have had 14 intercepted. With three games remaining, the Wildcats are within good range of the school record of 19 interceptions set in 1948.

The secondary foursome that has put the clamps on opposing passers consists of Rick Telander, Jack Dustin, Mike Coughlin, and Eric Hutchinson. Dustin, a product of Taft High School in Chicago, leads in interceptions with four while Hutchinson and Telander have three each.

Chicago Today
Why NU Scares Foes' QBs by Bill Jauss

November 6, 1970

You have to study Rick Telander, Jack Dustin, Eric Hutchinson and Mike Coughlin a long time before you realize why they provide Northwestern with the best secondary in college football.

Then it strikes you—as it did on one play last evening on the muddy, chilly, lighted Wildcats practice field.

The quarterback dropped back, faked a short pump and hurled a bull's-eye toward his flanker who was streaking down the left sideline on a "flag" route.

Telander, the right cornerback, never looked at the passer. He kept both eyes fixed on the flanker as both men sprinted side by side as close together as two guys in a phone booth.

The ball was right there. So was the defender. Three hands clutched for the spiral. Telander reached the ball first and tipped it away just before both men tumbled into the mud.

If Telander, a Peoria senior, or any of his three defensive backs pulls a play like this against Minnesota tomorrow, it will be applauded by some 40,000 Dyche Stadium fans.

Telander's "cheering section" last night consisted of secondary coach Rick Venturi and the three swift, smart juniors who help Rick form this unusual group.

Sticky man-to-man defense—a rarity in college ball—is at the heart of Northwestern's great record. The Cats play a man-to-man more than 80 percent of the time.

The Wildcats rank third in the nation. Their average passing yield of 85.9 yards a game puts them a shade behind Dartmouth (83.7) and Rice (84.8).

But neither Dartmouth nor Rice has played week by week against a succession of passers such as Notre Dame's Joe Theismann; Dennis Dummit,

UCLA; SMU's Chuck Hixon; Mike Wells of Illinois; Wisconsin's Neil Graf; Gary Danielson of Purdue, and Rex Kern of Ohio State.

The really remarkable statistic about the Wildcats is that they're holding these fine passers to a completion average of 32 percent.

How do they do it?

"Well, maybe we don't have any one superstar," Telander explained. "But we don't have a weak link, either. We're all fast. We've all been timed in 4.6 seconds for 40 yards. We're all pretty good basketball players and we can jump."

Playing pass defense, Telander said, is "studying teams' and players' patterns on film and then playing with 'controlled anticipation'...not blindly going for what you expect, but looking for it and still remaining ready to react."

The four pass thieves kid one another a lot, like joshing free safety Hutchinson for his droopy mustache and arguing which is the best basketball player.

"We try to keep loose," Telander said. "But we worry. Especially Dustin and me. We're on the corners and it's hard for us to get to sleep worrying about the men we'll have to cover."

The sleep part was true, for sure.

We stayed in a hotel the night before every game, home and away, and roomie Dustin and I would be keyed up and half nuts thinking about our assignments. At least, I would be.

Dustin would finally fall asleep, and I'd lie awake in my strange bed for what seemed like hours, my heart pounding. The thrill of the unknown—and whatever it might bring—lurked like a wavering vision. And not without reason.

Early in the Michigan State game, for instance, Dustin came to me in the huddle, his eyes wide.

"Jesus Christ, did you cover No. 1 yet!"

I just had.

"Who the hell is he?" Dustin asked in mortal fear.

"I don't know," I answered in equal terror. The guy had gone past me in a straight line of flame. "He's a blur. You don't know who he is?"

"No," said Dustin, looking ashen. "My God, I don't know."

It turned out he was tiny sprint champion Herb Washington, a track phenom wearing the look-at-me numeral "1" on his green jersey. He was a recent wideout addition to the Spartan team, a man who one day would be hired by George Steinbrenner to be the Yankees' designated base stealer in the World Series.

Old Herb had missed making our scouting report.

Which was why the sleep thing was true.

"Did you wear a jock?" Zack asks. He is 12.

"Hell, yes. Absolutely." I'm in the kitchen, watching *SportsCenter*. "Boo-yah!" was the last word I heard.

"See," says Judy. Something was under discussion. As usual I am, like my daughters' favorite movie, clueless.

"You have to wear one," says the wife.

"But it's too hard!" Zack whines. A set-to is coming. The conditions are right.

"For what?" I ask, involvement forced.

"Football, and I don't want to."

"Why?"

"The plastic thing hurts."

"What plastic thing?"

"The hard thing. You know!"

I spin away from the tube.

"That's a cup. The jock is the soft thing."

"Oh," says Zack.

STANDARD PLAYER CONTRACT
For
THE NATIONAL FOOTBALL LEAGUE
Between

Kansas City Chiefs Football Club, Inc., a Texas Corporation, hereinafter called "Club," which Club operates under the name and style of Kansas City Chiefs and which Club is presently a member of the National Football League, hereinafter called "League" and Rick Telander, hereinafter called "Player."

In consideration of the respective promises herein the parties agree as follows:...

3. For: the Player's services as a skilled football player during the term of this contract... the Club promises... to pay Player each football season during the term of this contract...the amount of $15,000.00 to be payable as follows: One-fourteenth of said amount following the playing of each regular season game...

As additional consideration for the execution of the contract above referred to and for the agreement of the Player to report for play and practice with the Club... the Club agrees to pay the Player the (bonus) sum of $3,000.00...

(Please refer to reverse side of contract for additional bonus provisions.)

*Player shall receive an additional bonus of $1,500.00 providing he is a member of the regular 40-man active roster as of September 19, 1971.

*Player shall receive an additional bonus of $2,500.00 providing he starts 7 regular league season games at his position during the regular league season.

*Player shall receive an additional bonus of $5,000.00 providing he is selected "Rookie of the Year" by the Newspaper Enterprises Association.

*Player shall receive an additional bonus of $2,500.00 providing he is selected to participate in the Pro Bowl following the regular 1971 season.

CLUB RULES AND REGULATIONS

1. All players must be on time for all meetings, practice sessions, meals, and all types of transportation. The curfew must be observed. Players must keep all publicity appointments and be on time.

2. Drinking of intoxicants is forbidden.

3. Players must not frequent gambling resorts nor associate with gamblers or other notorious characters.

4. Players must report all injuries to a coach and the club physician or trainer immediately.

5. Players must wear coats and neckties in hotel lobbies, public eating places, and on all public conveyances.

6. Players must familiarize themselves with their contract.

7. Players shall not write or sponsor magazine or newspaper articles, or endorse any product or service or appear on or participate in any radio or television program without the consent of the club.

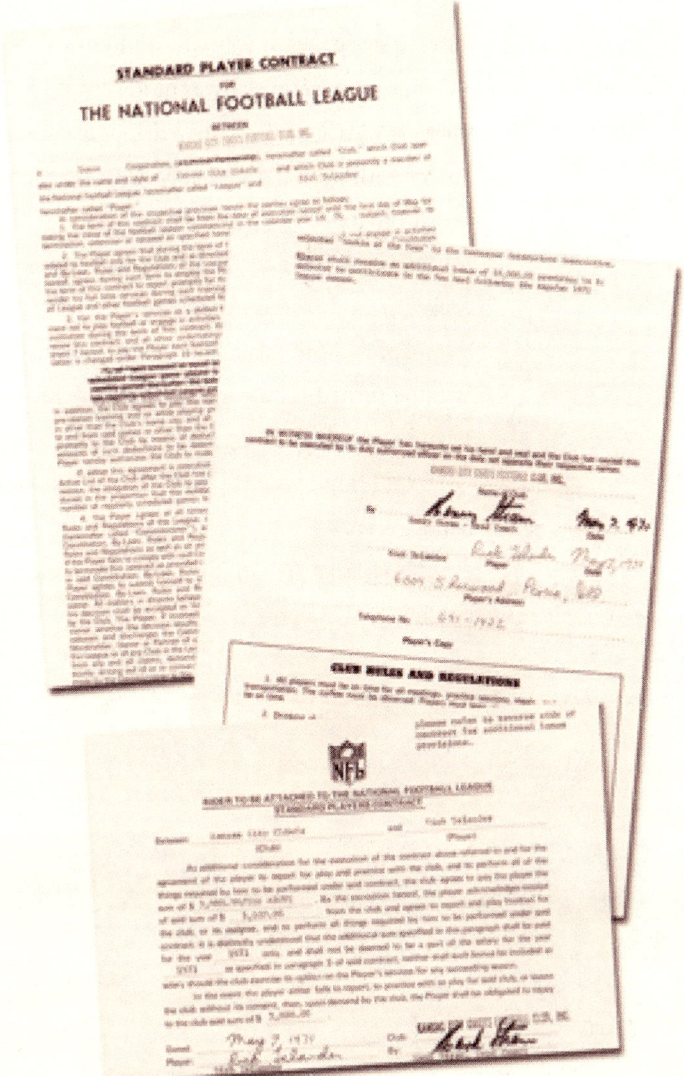
STANDARD PLAYER CONTRACT
THE NATIONAL FOOTBALL LEAGUE
CLUB RULES AND REGULATIONS
RIDER TO BE ATTACHED TO THE NATIONAL FOOTBALL LEAGUE
STANDARD PLAYERS CONTRACT

THINGS LEARNED FROM FOOTBALL:
One of the hardest and most important things in life is figuring out if you're hurt or just hurting.

There was a knock at the hotel door. I was in Los Angeles writing about the 2004 Rose Bowl for my newspaper. It was late, and I had ordered a Caesar salad because I was hungry, but I knew if I ordered what I wanted—a dripping cheeseburger with fries—I'd probably never sleep and I'd gain five pounds.

I opened the door and the room server walked in and placed the tray on the side table. He uncovered the salad, laid out the silver ware. Then he turned to me and said, "You're Rick Telander, aren't you?"

I told him I was. He smiled and held out his hand.

"I'm Clarke Zeman, the son of your old coach."

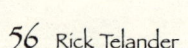

Halftime

My first piece in any publication anywhere, shortly before graduation—came in the *Daily Northwestern*, April 20, 1971. I was done with college practice. I was reflecting. I couldn't type a lick. So I wrote in longhand and my friend David Israel, the sports editor, typed for me:

Lots of things happen in the spring at Northwestern. Bikinis appear, Frisbees fly, new love affairs begin, old girlfriends are dumped, puppies sprout (man, there are dogs everywhere running and snorting; one in particular, a squatty, obnoxious part-beagle there is often seen wearing an Iowa license plate or striped necktie; be kind to him; he's harmless and comes from a broken family), classes are forgotten, riots are contemplated—it's a time for stretching winter-weary joints and doing foolish things.

Unless you're a football player. Then it's a little different.

If you play football, you go to the practice fields behind McGaw Hall and hit and offend and defend and tackle and prove your virility beyond anyone's doubt, while most students bask in the sun and smoke joints on the beach.

You get to labor and sweat. Others sit and vegetate.

It's very hard to play football in the spring, especially knowing that your first game is nearly six months away. You start thinking about that opener against Michigan, and the old adrenaline starts pulsing around. If you're lucky it will stop after four weeks; if not, it can go on for half a year. And that is very hard on the system.

But football is a game of controlled brutality and hard, cold facts—one being that if you are to have a good fall season, you need a complementary spring season.

This truism led one of my more sensitive football friends to bemoan his role as an April athlete.

"'I got a mind to stop living,' he said, 'and go shop for a tombstone instead.'"

Only his words were borrowed from B.B. King. The emotion was genuine.

Yes, practicing football while others practice hedonism can lead a person to some serious soul-searching. You begin to think things like, "What is it that makes me different from other young men? Do I wear the mark of Cain on my forehead? Or am I insane?"

In calmer moments you realize that it is not true—you are normal. It is only that you are willing to sacrifice some of your postadolescent time to become a good football player, part of a good football team. For some reason you have the desire to reach your potential as an athlete.

You may be against the war in Vietnam, you may dislike Richard Nixon, you may hate fascism, racism, and male chauvinism, and may possibly not even like your mother or your role as an establishment-defender; you may have a secret desire to eat brown rice, grow long hair and become a Zen Buddhist freak or a strung-out motorcycle grease jockey; you may or may not like or feel all these things, but you do, somewhere deep inside, want to excel at one thing in life—and that is football.

And maybe it's worth missing a few sunny days on the beach for that goal.

I was just 22 that spring. I was reminding myself of certain things, trying to stamp out my own doubts. I liked the semi-colon, I notice now.

But the spring before, my junior spring, had been full of real riots. They followed the Kent State massacre, the student killings at Jackson State. The war dwarfed all. Distrust reigned. Northwestern students took over commuter artery Sheridan Road, the street that ran directly through campus, blocked it off, lit fires, tore down the wrought-iron fences by the library and built a fearsome barricade, declared Northwestern a free state. One day I was playing my new cornerback position. The next day school had been cancelled. Shut down. No finals. No grades. No refunds. Everybody go home, said the administration, before somebody gets killed.

The squad and staff will be quartered at Eaton Hall on the campus of William Jewell College. The building is air-conditioned and very conveniently located to our practice area. The entire facility is ideal, so we know you will enjoy it to the fullest.

It is our policy not to permit wives at training camp. We recommend, however, that all married players bring their wives to Kansas City once the season gets underway. You can start making arrangements for them once you are relatively sure of making the squad. There are many nice housing facilities, so I am sure you will be able to locate suitable housing.

Your expenses for travel will be handled by the Kansas City Chiefs, as was explained in a previous letter. Cars will be permitted in training camp. All board and lodging in our camp will be paid for by the club. All players will receive per diem of $13 a day while you are in training camp. Veterans will be paid a proportionate amount for each exhibition game depending on your longevity.

Remember that you are being paid to practice as well as play. Make sure that you realize the importance of being in condition when you report. The responsibility of reporting in shape is strictly up to you. I suggest you follow carefully and systematically your individual strength and running program. It will enable you to go right into our running and contact work as soon as we open camp. You cannot afford to have any injury due to poor physical condition.

Hair was a big deal back then. Facial hair. Head hair. Long hair of any sort was not favored by those in positions of authority. Long hair was linked to an attitude, a defiance. Hippies had long hair. Old football players like Johnny Unitas had short hair. As always, it was those in the positions of authority whose rules counted.

My hair was longish but not too long. A bit of it hung out of my helmet in the back like a mud flap. I had wispy sideburns that weren't particularly notable. I don't think the coaches found me threatening or controversial in any way. But I'm not sure.

Pets and firearms? I left my half-breed beagle, Leo, at home with my parents. If I made the team, I could drive back and get him. Of course, what apartment owner would let him in? He was an excitable dog, one I had rescued from a man who was driving him to the Peoria animal shelter—end of the line—two summers earlier. The man stopped to ask directions while I was pulling weeds in front of my dad's office by the Illinois River, and I said, "I'll take him." When Leo let out his war cry that told the world a rabbit was nigh, it sounded like a mad bugler in a cathedral.

Years later while working on a story at the Chicago Bears preseason camp in Platteville, Wisconsin, I was standing in the dorm parking lot as Steve McMichael arrived. The defensive tackle climbed out of his car wearing shorts, sandals, a Hawaiian shirt, and sunglasses. In one hand he held a suitcase. In the other he held a bug-eyed, quivering Chihuahua. He kissed the dog and said, "It's OK, Killer."

Rules change.

Firearms? I remember when the football dorm called Bud Wilkinson Hall at the University of Oklahoma seemed to have more guns in it than a police armory. I was visiting Norman in the late 1980s, not long after one Sooner had shot another, and several players were in jail for various things. There was even a report that a running back named Buster Rimes had a machine gun at the dorm and had fired it from the roof.

I didn't own a gun in 1971. Still don't.

Like a Rose 65

When I was a junior in high school I was so skinny and self-conscious I wore thermal underwear under my pants to a formal dance so I wouldn't look frail. Football players couldn't be skinny the way I was.

The irony of those five meals a day I ate as a teenager haunt me. Like everyone else these days, I can look at a plate of spaghetti and gain another belt notch.

There was basketball and baseball and soccer and tennis and golf and volleyball and swimming and track. I played them all. But at a certain age, American boys, on the cusp of becoming men, want to play football. They walk down school hallways knocking each other into lockers. They punch each other in the arms. They wrestle. They trip each other and laugh when a trip-ee goes flying off in a heap into a lawn or a bush or whatever. They pounce on one another, and sometimes they actually get mad and fight for real. But on a playground, if boys are clustered together, something brutish like football will pop up.

And you want muscles for football. Muscles are strength. Strength is dominance. Dominance is god. And boys of a certain age would like to be gods.

Thursday, July 22

Today was the first real day of double practice sessions. We were timed in the forty yd. dash, and I had a disgusting 4.8. We ran on the field, in our football shoes, and my legs felt really weak and tired, but there's no excuse. Since there are 15 defensive backs in camp and eight of those are veterans from the league's best defensive secondary, if I want to make this team I can't afford such things as 4.8 forties.

E. J. Holub already has ice packs on his knees, and we haven't even done anything. His knees look like roadmaps of Texas from his nine operations.

My roommate Mike Montgomery is a decent guy. He's strictly a safety, since he's not very fast at all, in my opinion. Our room isn't bad, nothing much, either. He's got his bed and his suitcase and I've got mine. He's from Southwest Texas State and he likes to lie back on his bed and read a cowboy book. Sometimes I'll play my guitar, but mostly I have other things on my mind, so I let it sit in its old case in the corner. I picked up Mike's book from the table and looked at it for a while, with its Old West cover and a cowboy on a horse like from *Gunsmoke*. It made me think that here I am a college grad who majored in English literature and I didn't bring anything with me to read. All I have now is a playbook with more diagrams than you can imagine.

I stop and close the notebook. I smile. What a silly little thing. "The Spiral Notebook," it says on its pea green cover. Cost: 15 cents. Thirty-two pages, "6 in. x 4 in." each. Why didn't I buy a bigger notebook? For such a major event in my life? I was cheap and on a young man's budget, but I think I could have afforded, say, a 50-cent extravaganza. I remember none of this, can't explain why some pages are done in red ink and some in black, why there are a couple of even smaller pages from another notebook stuck within.

I flip forward. Near the end of my little book there is writing in pencil: *Otis Taylor is one example of the tremendous athletic power on this team. He can put his elbows on the goalpost.* And even blue ink: *No pads. Wilbur Young, 317 lbs.* I remember my affection in grammar school for different colored inks, particularly for those pens that held several colors in one barrel. Playing with them and doodling during class helped keep me sane. But this notebook variety, I am certain, came out of necessity. I wrote when I could, with what I could.

And as I think about it, I feel certain I know why I bought such a tiny diary. It was audacious to think I could be an NFL player. But it was preposterous to think I could be a writer. Bill Gleason was one man, making an idle comment. *The Daily Northwestern.* One column, typed by a pal. Who was I? Who, on this planet, did I think I was writing for?

Thus, the secretiveness, the smallness, the unobtrusiveness. Even my entries were brief. The miniature notebook drew no attention to itself. It could be hidden away, torn to pieces in a moment and discarded.

Like my dreams.

How about this photo?

Here it is in the dusty box, and it is an illusion. I look at it closely. Whose leg is that? There is Rex Kern in front of a blurred crowd, the football cocked in his right arm, his mouth wide open, a look of terror on his face. It appears that he has three legs. But no, that leg to the left is a defender's, a hidden player stealing up from behind. It is mine.

I look closely and there is my left hand gripping Kern's left shoulder from behind just lightly enough that his shoulder pads have been yanked back slightly, and his white Buckeyes jersey is tight but not yet choking him. Why his look of horror?

Shock.

Premonition.

Faded almost into gray with the crowd—camouflaged is the word—is my right hand, a fly wink from slamming down on Kern's throwing shoulder. The elusive Ohio State quarterback had scrambled, and I was on a delayed blitz from the right corner and he couldn't see me, and he was toast. I remember the play well. I was a junior. The game was at home. I dug my fingers into his pads and threw him down as hard as I could, as the ball sailed incomplete. Kern hurt his shoulder and had to leave the game.

I'm not going to lie about this. There is no reason at this stage in my life. Football speaks to something basic within the male system, to the testosterone and dark cave principles that drip through the crania and loins of our half of the species.

I felt great.

Speed is extremely important to us. Be prepared to take full sprints the first day. You will be timed in the 40-yard dash. Our decision in keeping men will be made strictly in accordance with what we feel will best help the Kansas City Chiefs. Reputation means nothing when it comes to making this football team. To make our squad you must be in top physical condition and earn the right to be a member of our 40-man team. It will be a tough, competitive fight, and only those who are willing to sacrifice and discipline themselves, both mentally and physically, will survive. These are the principles that we value in football.

We have been working diligently since the first of April, but we must continue to push. The latter part of June and July must be our most productive months, so it's

imperative that you lift weights with renewed determination, and follow your strength and running program to the letter. As of July 1, add ten 40-yard sprints to your individual program.

My first mini-camp had been a curious affair. There were lots of us new players walking around, trying to learn the Chiefs' "system." The old-timers didn't seem to care much about the practices, but they had a kind of careful alertness when huddles were formed, coaches spoke, announcements were made, a rookie made a nice play.

A lot of the veterans bitched quietly to one another about the weightlifting that was required. There were spanking new—and newly invented—Nautilus machines set up past the end zone of one of the fields, and some of the rotations one's joints had to perform to do the exercises did not mesh well with old injuries and old age. I myself did boundless reps on the shoulder derotation machine, among others, and a day later I could barely raise my arms.

Weightlifting was new school. The vets were old school. They grumbled because they knew weight training was effective and here to stay.

The Chiefs had always been the most modern of teams, with Stram's "floating pocket" offense, his famous "stack defense," the reliance on speed and technical innovation, and the studied recruitment of black players from small, all-black schools, or anywhere, in an era when many major college and NFL teams were still whiter than napkins. But progress, by definition, never ends. And there was no comfort in that for the men who had already succeeded with the earlier "progress."

What I sensed above all was that pro football is a team game, but if you as an individual didn't make the team, nothing else mattered. College was dead.

I called Bob Zeman when I got home from Los Angeles. He and his wife had retired to Las Vegas after Bob's years of coaching and private business ventures, and they were taking it easy. Bob was in good shape and he was thrilled that his son had stumbled into me in such an unlikely way and given me his dad's phone number. Clarke was trying his hand at the movie biz, Zeman told me, and I told him I wished Clarke only the best.

We chatted for some time, and it was fine, indeed, to hear his voice. He mentioned the Dave thing, and we both had a good laugh over that.

Then I asked him again about being prepared and calm and accepting.

"You know, all my life I've had my guys go through situations in their minds before the snap," he replied. "'What do I do if it's a pass?' 'What do I do if it's a run?' Before the play occurs, you've already thought it through in your mind and you're not confused. *I* used to get confused as a player, so I'd say, 'How can I settle myself down?'"

What else?

"Well then, of course, you must realize the opponent is going to complete some passes on you. You know it will happen, and you know it's OK.. And you move on."

THINGS LEARNED FROM FOOTBALL:

There are times later in life when you remember how miserable you once were, during the heat, the filth, the exhaustion, the pain. They remind you that you can do this thing now.

Third Quarter

Jack Rudnay has been my pal. He asked me to come and have a few beers at the local joint—something rookies don't do. So I went and sat with him and Ed Lothamer and Jim Lynch and Ed Podolak and drank a few beers. I'm so eager for anything that comes from the veterans' mouths that I must seem like a starved dog.

Jim Otis likes Woody Hayes. Calls him a GREAT coach. I had to chuckle after hearing some Hayes stories from Mike Sensibaugh and Bruce Jankowski. They're both from Ohio State. Sensibaugh was drafted with me in the eighth round, and Bruce I think was No. 10. I remember covering Bruce when we played at Ohio Stadium and how he had a big bandage on his forehead. One of my Northwestern teammates told me something happened on one of the kickoffs or something and Bruce got clobbered and his head split open. I hate even thinking about that game, even though I played pretty well and had those two interceptions off Kern. Ohio State had the worst patterns I'd ever seen. If we'd won, we would have gone to the Rose Bowl, but then, the season would have dragged on and on. Can't think about it.

Anyway, they told me stories about Woody, about him smashing movie projectors, punching himself in the head, driving a tractor through the doors of a locked room.

Ed Lothamer said he almost died from nervousness, anxiety, and high blood pressure when he skipped a year of football.

"I had blood pressure of 220 over 180 and the doc said my head was gonna blow off. So I'm back and I'm enjoying it and just taking it easy. I mean, it's no big deal if Mo Moorman can beat me on pass blocking, you know. What does that really mean?"

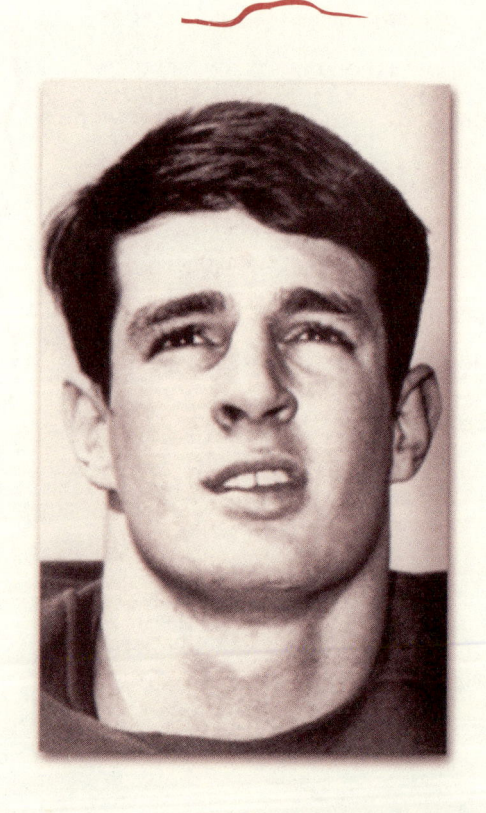

The nine-year-old stuff is long gone, and now Zack is 12 and wants to play on the junior high heavyweight football team. But he is skinny the way I was skinny as a kid, maybe skinnier. He looks like an arrow. He is 5-9, weighs only 123 pounds, and should be a lightweight, for which the cutoff is 130. But if he plays with the lightweights, he will have to be a lineman. As a heavy, he will be perhaps the lightest kid in the league, but he'll be able to run with the ball or catch it, and play strong safety, which is all he wants to do.

I don't know if I want him to play at all. And yet, I am proud that he wants to. As ever, I am conflicted.

**NORTHWESTERN FOOTBALL MAGAZINE
—50 CENTS
Northwestern vs. Wisconsin
N Men's Day/ Dyche Stadium/ October 18, 1969
"MEET THE WILDCATS—OUT OF UNIFORM"
RICK TELANDER DB/ Peoria, Ill.**—Paints and plays the guitar...made seven-week, 10,000-mile drive around country last summer on $100...worked at carnivals, picking grapes and baling hay...named outstanding man in freshman class two years ago.

That trip was wild.

My buddy Bill Blair, my neighborhood pal since second grade who worked with me at the cemetery, was my fellow road warrior on the journey. We headed north through Wisconsin and Minnesota into Canada, then west to the Pacific Ocean, then south to Mexico, then east 3,000 miles to Florida and Jekyll Island, Georgia, where we hung out a few days near my grandparent's old home, then up the East Coast to Washington, D.C., Pennsylvania, and New York and back into Canada, before coming down through Michigan and Indiana to Peoria. All of it in my 1961 Volkswagen camper that had a top speed—I kid you not—of 46 miles per hour. We could hit the mid-fifties coming down a hill. Sixty or better coming down a mountain. But going west across Canada, on narrow, sometimes gravel highways, into the prevailing wind, we did upper thirties for days. Sometimes the road was so straight and empty that as I drove I laid out cards on the dashboard and played solitaire.

Part of the problem was that we had my green, racing-striped, ten-foot-six-inch longboard strapped to the roof of the van. At one point deep in the Manitoba plains, Blair estimated we were farther from surfable water than we were from the Northwest Territories. Outside Moose Jaw a man asked us if we were transporting an airplane wing.

The good part was we were able to surf on two different oceans in the same trip. We drove through snow in the Idaho Rockies, watched our peanut butter turn to liquid in Arizona, captured a tarantula near El Paso and kept it as a pet, watched the first man walk on the moon from Dallas, and drove within miles of Woodstock without even knowing the greatest concert in rock history was taking place.

But I had a football with me, and football shoes, and what I remember is always thinking about the season ahead. We would park for the night on back roads, next to farm fields or a state park or a river bank. And I would break out the ball and punt it and run after it and play catch with Blair and do pushups and sprints and backpedals. Sometimes, such as after we hoed beets in what seemed like an inland desert near Yakima, Washington, then showered at the local YMCA, I ate my hot dogs at our campfire and collapsed onto my sleeping bag, wasted for the duration. But football was always there.

It loomed big and bright and portentous as the July moon.

"Tom?"

"Yes."

"Tom Peeler?"

"Yes."

"You, you sound just the same! It's your old quarterback, Rick Telander."

"Well, how *are* you?"

"Great! You sound great, too!"

"You probably thought I was 70 back when I was coaching."

"You probably thought I was 12."

We laugh. We chat.

"Can we get together some time, do you think? Just to talk about football and stuff. Are you still in Peoria?"

"Same house. Sure, I'd love to."

One of his four sons is transferring from a marine base on the East Coast, he tells me. And he has a teenaged granddaughter visiting for the summer, and, then, darn it, he's having a hip replacement in a week. So there's a lot going on.

"I'll drive down if it's OK. I can get there in three or four hours. If you think it's OK. I could even come down Wednesday."

"Wednesday's fine."

I drive slowly past my old high school. It doesn't look dilapidated, but it doesn't look crisp and modern as it did when I was a student there so long ago. Most of the windows in every classroom have been walled over. For security? Energy savings? Or is it to keep students, such as this one-time boy, from gazing blankly, distantly, longingly at the fields of grass that surround the building?

A bit farther down the road, and then I turn left into the subdivision that once was so barren, but now has mature trees in every lawn. The houses are modest, small even, and there on

Like a Rose 83

Cimarron Drive is my old coach's. I know it's the correct address, because he told me twice. But how strange. I have never been here before. I couldn't imagine visiting a coach at his house. To see his chairs, his kitchen?

I park in front. I look up the steep front yard at the split-level house with the garage door facing me. I haven't seen Tom Peeler in 36 years. I feel nervous. I am his old quarterback once again, not the receiver I was at the start of high school and college, not the cornerback I became, or the strong safety with the Chiefs. I am not even the man with four children and a wife and a career. I am the high school quarterback. The one he made.

We sit on the couch in the small living room. Coach Peeler's wife of 53 years, Mary Anne, smiles and offers us milk and chocolate chip cookies. There is a sleeping mongrel dog on the floor, name of Annabelle. Peeler's 48-year-old son Jeff is here from New Jersey, as are a grandson and two granddaughters.

We make small talk and then folks leave us alone.

OBSERVER

Volume IV, Number 16   Thursday, September 16, 1965   Single Copy 10¢

I look at my old coach. Except for being bald on top he hasn't changed at all. He's tall, maybe two inches taller than I, and except for a small belly, country lean. I know he was a good athlete himself, even earned a basketball scholarship to Southeast Missouri State in Cape Girardeau, Missouri. I recall a photo from the summer of 1965, of him and me and the starting Richwoods quarterback that year, John Hostetler, on the cover of a Peoria community newspaper called *The Observer*. I am a bony, 16-year-old, junior wide receiver-to-be and Hostetler is our senior, cannon-armed leader who will be off to the Air Force Academy in a year. Peeler is stoic, bespectacled, kneeling between us, holding a football like an offering. His eyes are hidden in the shadow of his ball cap. Back then I thought he was older than dirt. Funny, he was just 35. He's 74 now. Been retired as a coach since 1984, as a teacher since 1990. He still loves to hunt, still loves to fish.

"Remember how I'd give you boys Labor Day weekend off during two-a-days? So you could recuperate?" he asks with a chuckle. "What it actually was, I'd go off to Effingham to hunt with my father-in-law. Soon as Saturday practice was over—[he claps his hands, Bang!]—Maryanne and I took off. Hunt doves in the afternoon, squirrels the rest of the time."

I laugh. Jeez, I don't remember any time off.

This is so nice seeing Coach after so many years. I look at him and the old memories swarm back—the zits, the hallways, the bells clanging the next class, the big games.

"Coach, I drive 200 miles and you didn't bother to tell me what you'll be wearing?"

He looks at himself, at me. We both have on black golf shirts, light shorts, brown belts, white socks, sneakers. We look like separated idiot twins. Another round of guffaws.

We dive into the old memories. He's a southern Illinois rural guy, of course, with a twang from the hills and fields not too far above Kentucky. He's from Anna, actually, 21 miles south of Carbondale. I ask him about sports down there, where there's a basketball-mad town called Cobden, with a team called the Appleknockers.

"We played Cobden," he says. "At the time it had the widest main street in America. Big

Like a Rose *87*

street, then railroad tracks, then more street. Anyway, you wondered about their home court. A rim's only so big, but our team was warming up, and two balls got wedged in there. Of course, our own home court at Anna-Jonesboro High was so small it had two center lines."

Peeler was a tough offensive lineman, too, and his junior year his high school football team went undefeated. His senior year the team was undefeated, untied, and unscored upon until the second to the last game against Murfreesboro. That's when Peeler learned a major life lesson.

"We were supposed to play on a Friday night, and it rained so hard, and we were all in the locker room, fired up, ready to go, and our coach comes in and says, "Boys, the game is postponed till tomorrow." I asked him about it, and he said it was his decision. Well, on Saturday we lost 14-0. We were better than Murfreesboro. We played Johnson City in our last game and beat them, like, 52-0, and Murfreesboro had struggled against them. It was all mental. Our edge. Right then and there I made the decision that if I was ever a head coach that never will I postpone a game. We'll play her now."

Seldom do athletes, coaches, or anyone in sports get out at the right time, on their terms. But Tom Peeler did. With the youngest of his four sons, Greg, playing quarterback and middle linebacker, Peeler's 1984 Knights went undefeated and won the Illinois state 5-A Championship. Their title game was against Deerfield, but the semifinal game was the key. That was against perennial power Joliet Catholic, a school that has produced NFL standouts such as Mike Alstott and Tom Thayer. Richwoods played Joliet Catholic in a deluge--"When I left the stadium, there was water standing from the sideline to the hashmarks," says Peeler, but his only thought was, "We will not postpone the game!"

Then it was over. He taught history for six more years, but he was spent.

"I got intolerant there at the end," he says, shifting his weight restlessly in his stuffed chair. That hip. "I got inflexible. Looking back, you know what I really liked? No, not liked. I *loved* the practice field. Way more than games. Like that photo of you and John, there we are out on the field, and that is what I loved. Didn't matter if I had a good team or not. And that last year, why I wasn't interested that much. I couldn't make myself be. And I knew it was over."

He had already done so much. In his low-key but intense way he had coached so many more winning teams than losing teams, it was ridiculous. He coached Canton High School—the Little Giants, for God's sake—to an undefeated season. I have come back to him, I realize, because to me he is Gandalf, Merlin, the Obi-Wan Kenobi who gave me skill and confidence and power. But to himself, he was always the doubter. I find this fascinating. My pillar, my rock—had fissures. I was stunned to hear him say he only got into coaching because a friend in college said take Phys. Ed., and he only became a history teacher because another friend said take history.

"I'm at Cape State, as we called it, and I had no idea what I wanted to be." He smiles. I smiled too. I'm trying to imagine Tom Peeler directionless. "Anyway, when I really knew it was time to go was when we were getting ready to play Springfield South East, and they were *terrible*, and I thought about forfeiting the game."

Whoa, this was in the 13-0, state championship season. This was the Richwoods steamroller.

"I just wasn't interested. But we played, and my son Greg got hurt in the game. And I realized that when he wasn't at practice I wasn't enthused at all."

"So what was your motivation through the previous years?"

"Honestly? Truly? It was when our coaching staff would say, 'Here is a kid who will never,

ever play for us.' You know, I never cut anybody. And to see a kid who had nothing at all grow and work and stick it out and finally *play*—that was it.

"I think of Craig Williams. Remember ol' Smokey? As a freshman he didn't play. As a sophomore he didn't play. As a junior he played a bit. As a senior he was All-Conference."

I was All-Conference as a senior, too.

I wonder.

Somehow I am now an assistant coach for Zack's football team. Before I took the three-afternoons-a-week volunteer job, I watched one practice from my car, reading newspapers. Then, two days later, on a gorgeous afternoon, I watched while seated under a tree, mesmerized by the smell, the light, the ritualized machinations of this hormonal coming-out party before me.

"Hey, Mr. Telander," said one of the rec-center staff members pleasantly, startling me in mid-reverie. That was all it took to sign me up.

Zack was offered jersey number 34 for the heavyweight league, but he said no and took 33. "Thirty-four's Walter Payton's number," he told me when I asked why. "He was too good."

Friday, July 23

Old Hank must have called the sun in for this afternoon's practice. It was like a steam bath on the field from the heat and moisture lying in stagnant pools. Sometimes it felt like you were breathing the same air over and over, and the sweat on your arms reappeared in the same little beads no matter how many times you wiped them dry with a towel.

I was thinking to myself how similar we were to lunatics who run around in their winter clothes in July heat, because actually to cool off all we had to do was take off our 20 pounds of gear—helmets, shoulder pads, etc. And we would be much cooler also if we could practice when the sun isn't right overhead.

Well, discipline is the excuse for this madness.

The person who most fits his name—Charles Roundtree. His head is round, smooth, and shaved like a bowling ball, and his body resembles a bowl of chocolate pudding. The poor guy is so fat that he labors just to make it through calisthenics.

He smiles all the time and tries to take it casually when Warren McVea and Wendell Holmes start razzing him. "Wha's happnin', Tree?" they say continually and then burst into fits of laughter. Frank Pitts, too. He laughs so much and so insanely, they call him the Riddler. Well, I guess hazing is part of being a rookie, but being an obvious target for tirades of laughter is tough, no matter what the circumstances. Hang in there, Tree.

Honeybear—that's Willie Lanier—is also known as "Contact" for reasons that even a moron could not miss. He looks so nice and happy and cuddly like a big bear that like many great football players his transition on the field leaves you amazed. His helmet is padded on the outside, probably to prevent him from killing someone with one blow from his head. He has already caromed into Gene Thomas, a big fullback, and nearly broke the fellow's neck for him. I sleep better knowing he's on my side.

Winning three American Football League championships and a world championship was a fulfillment of a tremendous challenge and a great achievement. We have a rich, winning tradition. We established this tradition by hard work, second effort, self discipline, dedication, personal sacrifice, teamwork, and believing in our own ability and the ability of each other. Our goal and purpose in 1971 must be to recapture the championship of the world.

This will be a great challenge, so you must prepare yourself to meet it. Winning and success do not come easy. You must earn the right to enjoy it and be willing to make every personal sacrifice necessary for its achievement. I sincerely feel that we have the physical equipment, but ability alone is not enough. We must consistently express a fierce burning desire and a strong positive attitude each day of the season.

Consistency of attitude, emotions and execution are the keys to winning championships. Remember, too, that there's no mystery to being a great football team. It is still a game of blocking, tackling and artistic excellence. Great teams don't do extraordinarily things, they just do the ordinary things extraordinarily well.

I will look forward to seeing you soon. Work hard, don't be fat, and be ready for a hell of a training camp.

Kindest regards,
"Hank"
Henry Stram,
Head Coach

Jeff Peeler comes into the room. Like all his brothers he had a career in the military. But a few years ago he got out, moved to New Jersey and started work as a tax accountant headquartered in Building Number 2 of the World Trade Center in lower Manhattan. On September 11, 2001, Jeff's morning train was delayed, and he watched from Hoboken as the twin buildings with many of his colleagues inside crashed to the earth like a pair of skeletons crumbling to ash.

Jeff isn't over it. Nor will he ever be. But life goes on. This is the house where he was raised. This is where he and his brothers can always find comfort.

"Dad," he says, looking out the window at the front yard, "you have a wonderful gift for planting trees crooked."

The old coach shifts again, winces with the dysfunctional joint that soon will be replaced, and chuckles. Jeff leaves, and Peeler says, "People said when the first three boys were little and cute and blond-headed, 'Enjoy 'em now, because they'll be teenagers soon!' Well, I enjoyed them then, and as they got older, and Greg came along, I enjoyed them more. They became my best friends. All of them. If they lived here now, they'd still be my best friends. Two main things I taught them: I want you to know I love your mother, and don't be bullies. Don't let people pick on you, now. Defend yourself. Get kicked out of school for defending yourself? We'll both take a day off."

The coach gestures, and something catches my eye. Or rather, the lack of something. He has no wedding band on his left ring finger. Indeed, he has no left ring finger at all. I had forgotten about that. I noticed it when he was showing me all the quarterback moves way back when. It made him seem lordly and mysterious and profound. But soon it was irrelevant. Lost it in the army, he says now, looking at the stump. Climbing a rock. Wedding band got it. Life.

Mary Anne reappears, and this time we *will* eat the cookies and drink the milk. I mention that I feel like a guest at Ward and June Cleaver's house, and they both smile in polite agreement. But I realize they have no idea what I'm talking about. They read books more than they watch TV, and anyway, he's a damn coach.

November 28, 1970

THINGS LEARNED FROM FOOTBALL:
There is at least one moment in each game when you feel certain you can hear the sound of your own frenzy.

Chicago Tribune

Northwestern, which surprised many experts by finishing in a tie for second place in the Big Ten with a 6-1 record, was the No. 1 defensive team in the conference, according to statistics released yesterday.

The Wildcats yielded only 215.6 yards per game, and opponents were able to gain but 57.7 yards per contest passing. Northwestern's outstanding secondary of Rick Telander, Eric Hutchinson, Jack Dustin and Mike Coughlin permitted Big Ten foes to complete a paltry 28.2 percent of their passes.

Nationally, the Wildcats' pass defense ranked only behind Toledo in yards yielded passing, 79.3 to 77.8. But Northwestern had a lower percentage yield, .319 to .351 and faced stiffer competition.

Fourth Quarter

Saturday, July 24

Woke up this morning in the middle of an absurd dream about a wrong phone number because of war beats. The great throbbing percussion turned out to be one of the madman managers beating on everyone's doors. Six-thirty in the morning and they force you to eat breakfast when all you can think about is sleep—glorious, blessed, forgetful sleep in which you live in another world devoid of football (although no less distorted and strange).

Hank got out the banana peel early this morning and "slid a few people out of town," as he calls it. Poor Charles Roundtree is gone, as well as Arnold Blancus, James Whitaker, Dan Klepper, and Alvin Hawes. Names soon to be relegated to the limitless realms of obscurity.

"Why'd they can old Tree?" my roomie asked me.

"Because he was a fat piece of shit," I replied, of course bringing on gales of laughter.

It's not that we're cruel and heartless, rather it's the knowing that we all are in the same dangling situation and to laugh at someone's misery which could just as easily have been ours is the only way we can confront the situation. We can either laugh or cry.

Some people's nerves are getting very bad.

Sunday, July 25

Heat and sweat. I'm getting to know each very well.

Old Henry is playing with our minds. Using the strategy of brainwashing, he has taken away all of our normal privileges and then gives a few back as if from kindness and understanding. Sly bastard.

And I know, yes indeed, I am positive that Mr. Stram, our head coach and brainwasher, wears a toupee. He can't fool me because I know that no man's real hair looks like that—all slick and perfect.

The Riddler has one of the most incredible laughs I have ever heard. Very high and staccato like a woodpecker or something.

It's fifty dollars a pound for being overweight. The heavy guys are wearing every imaginable kind of rubber suit.

Monday, July 26

My roommate is a good example of the diversity on this team. He's my age and he plays defensive back, but after that the similarities stop. He's from west Texas and he's married with a two-year-old boy, and he is the closest thing to a real cowboy I've ever met.

When I came in one day and he was drinking from a Coke cup and I asked him for a swig and he said, "Aw, you don't want

Like a Rose 103

a slug of tobacco juice, do you?" I realized we had a few cultural differences.

So I asked him about home and he described it as a place where "you can see for two weeks," and where every morning you got up at 6:30 to ride your horse out onto the range and tend to ranching business.

"Well, I generally go to bed around 10:00 if there's nothing happening," he told me when I wondered how he rose so easily at 6:30 for our mandatory breakfast. "And there's generally nothing happening," he added.

He and his best friend own a cattle ranch back in the plains, and a star rising over the flat Missouri corn fields can start him longing for home and the freedom of open spaces, horses, and the honest rewards of ranching.

He looked at me the other day and said, "Rick, what in the world am I doing here?"

His meaning was much the same as everyone else's meaning when they question their reasons for playing in the violent, insecure, nerve-wracking world of football instead of tending to the normal duties at home. I can't answer them because I often ask myself the same question.

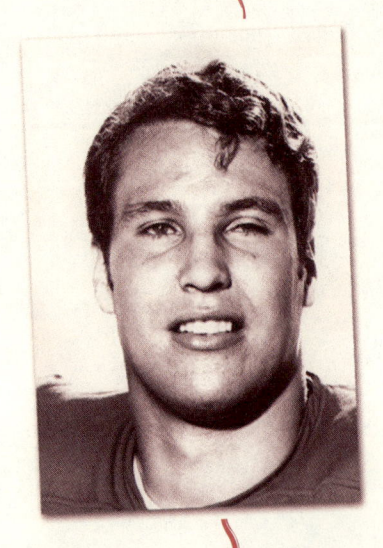

Mike Oriard was a backup offensive lineman when I was with the Chiefs. I didn't know him, but I recognized him as a former Notre Dame player, one year ahead of me. I would see him occasionally in the food line at the William Jewell cafeteria or running off to his O-line drills with the other behemoths. He was tall, relatively slender for his position, quiet, and had a thick shock of wavy dark hair.

Years later I would find that Oriard was, like myself, an English literature enthusiast, a writer, and then, after his seven years in the NFL, a professor of English at Oregon State University. One day I happened upon an essay Oriard had written on the essence of football. He made the fascinating point that football, a game in which young men had once died in stunning numbers in the early part of the twentieth century, should be made safe, but not too safe.

The possibility of injury—even severe injury—on any play was the very key to the game. If you couldn't get hurt, if you didn't stand the chance of hurting someone else, Oriard was saying, why play at all?

I thought about that. The professor was correct.

Tuesday, July 27

Drank with Lenny Dawson, Johnny Robinson and the Duck at their bar. It was all right, but I didn't get to bed until 12:00 or so.

They told a million drinking and skirt-chasing stories. Shocked my ass off it did.

Wednesday, July 28

Willie Mitchell is a panic. He walks around shouting out drill cadences and marching in mock army routines. He's deadpan all the way, sort of reminds me of my old pal Jay Petran from grade school days.

I got real lonesome this morning when I walked out and heard a mourning dove singing in the drizzle. Reminded me of home and those long-gone days of innocence, whether real or imagined, days when you didn't get up at 6:30 in the morning to eat breakfast with 270-pound men with muscles

Like a Rose

the size of gorillas'. Football definitely has brought a new dimension into my life—winning, losing, fearing to lose, competition with all things in a sort of maniacal race to be the best. I find it hard to live in harmony with my surroundings sometimes, simply because I feel I either must dominate or be beaten. Winner or loser, that's all there is in football.

The afternoon has gone by in a haze of good cheer. I have told Coach all about my work and family and this old Kansas City diary I found. And he has told me, for instance, that he always hated—*hated*—the kicking game. I was the Richwoods punter, and I can vouch that we hardly ever practiced that part of the game. It's amusing, I tell him, because I understand precisely why he found the kicking stuff so dull. It wasn't really football at all.

But now, I ask him politely, why did he make me the quarterback?

He nods his head, as though he's been waiting to answer this for a long time.

Some of the things the players do in the off season are amazing. Some of them go the big business route with their own car dealerships, restaurants, or bars and pretend that their money comes from these sources of revenue.

Others attend to their hobbies. Fishing and loafing and playing golf probably come in first place, with guys like Dave Hill, Willie Mitchell and the like. Drinking takes the No. 1 spot for such as Jerrel Wilson and Mike Livingston.

The Riddler, of all people, owns a florist shop. I can picture him walking through rows of flowers and potted plants, laughing as if the whole world were a joke, suddenly snatching a petal here or there, putting it in his buttonhole and collapsing again in avalanches of laughter.

Some of the players, I'm sure, just sit around and count their money.

Thursday, July 29

The rain made things sloppy and incredibly cold for this time of year—a low of 55 degrees is expected tonight. Practices without the usual heat and humidity are very easy, something I am very grateful to someone for. I don't know who, just someone.

Emmitt Thomas tells us (me and Mike) that you never know what can happen as far as making the team. "It's all being in the right place at the right time; not just talent."

**11th Annual Coaches' All-America Game
Media Guide
Jones Stadium Texas Tech University
Lubbock, Texas June 26, 1971
The East Squad**

Rick Telander, Def. Back, 6-2, 192, Northwestern (Kansas City)—A veteran in Northwestern's secondary that led the nation, limiting completion average of opposing passers to 32 percent. All-Big Ten Academic both as junior and senior. Shifted to defensive backfield after sophomore season as a split end. **Was a guest columnist for the *Daily Northwestern*, Northwestern's student newspaper.**

What did I know about writing? Almost nothing. But I read and I read. Reading was simply the inverse of writing, I skipped classes, dozens of classes--but I read books. I read all the books. There were the great novels by Hemingway and Tolstoy and Fitzgerald and Dostoevsky and Stendahl and Dickens. I was punished in a high school German class when I was caught reading Hugo's *Toilers of the Sea* behind my German grammar book. But I read and read. Authors said the things I felt. And they felt things I could only think.

There was my favorite writer, from no class ever assigned—Henry Miller. He came from nowhere. He was nuts. He had nothing, owned nothing, lived like a joyful pilgrim while all around him things fell apart. He was ecstatic in his chaos. There in Paris he sat on a bench, penniless, love-lost, without prospects or hope, smiling as he watched the Seine flow to the sea, the happiest man in the world. It all was good, even the bad, he said—the hunger and the rejection and the loss and the sadness and the struggle and even the dying. Nothing lasted. But there was ecstasy in the living. It was transcendentalism, partying, the Whitman-esque barbaric yawp, the glimmer of the release that the Eastern mystics spoke of, the peace that could be discerned in the maddening smile of the Buddha. There was release in opening your arms. Accepting the collision.

So I practiced my writing. And I looked for writers who were athletes, who were manly and would have loved football. Or did love it. Hemingway was a tough guy. He was big, over six feet tall, fancied himself a fighter. He had been wounded in World War I. He fished. He drank. He stood up when he typed.

There was Jack Kerouac, the frenzied Zen traveler with amphetamine pal Neal Cassidy, tearing up the open road in search of enlightenment. Kerouac had been an All-State running back in Massachusetts before badly injuring his knee at Columbia. There was legal scholar Byron "Whizzer" White, a Heisman Trophy winner and Supreme Court justice. There was triple-Pulitzer Prize-winning poet and college athlete Archibald MacLeish, whom a rival coach once called, "the dirtiest little son-of-a-bitch center to ever play for Yale."

These were some of my guys. They knew what was out there on the field.

Political writer George Will was in town, and he and I were sitting down for a beer at, of all places, Mike Ditka's Bar & Grille. Will, originally from Champaign, Illinois, is a maniacal baseball fan. Worse than that, he is a Cubs fan.

I asked him why he wasn't a Bears fan, a football fan.

"Football combines the two worst components of American life," he sniffed. "Violence and committee meetings."

I pondered that.

"Baseball combines two worse than that," I said. "Fake fights and rainouts."

Friday, July 30

I remember squinting and looking up at the sun. Coach Stram was up on his tower.

"Don't let that happen, Rick," this voice said. It was his, but I could barely see him. He was like part of the sun. "If a man breaks down your cushion, deliver a blow. Knock him off balance. Neutralize him."

Stram was talking about the play before, in which I'd let tight end Morris Stroud get too close to me and had been beaten on a post-flag pattern. Morris stands 6-10 and weighs 250, and he's got good speed and tremendous jumping ability. Somebody told me that in last year's Oakland game he was back at the goal line and missed only by inches of blocking George Blanda's last field goal, a kick that cleared the cross bar by three feet.

"Yes sir," I said to the sun-hidden voice.

The air was thick with hot moisture, and as I tried to catch my breath it seemed like I was re-breathing the same stagnant pools each time. What I wanted to say was, "Why don't you come down and neutralize this big bastard!"

The sweat seemed to crawl down my arms like ants. Wipe them away, they came right back. God, I hate the heat!

I had to work harder. In the shimmering air Stroud looked like Goliath incarnate. Is everybody on this team a freak?

How about Jim Hines? He set the world record in the 100 meter dash at the Mexico Olympics, and now he's a wide receiver.

I watched Kerry Reardon cover Hines in one of our drills. He did OK. But as we lined up and you could see who you would have to cover, I stopped to tie my shoelace so I could avoid Hines. It wouldn't matter what he did, I'd just run deep.

> THINGS LEARNED FROM FOOTBALL:
> Confidence is just arrogance with reason.

Overtime

**NORTHWESTERN FOOTBALL
MEDIA GUIDE 1968**

**Telander, Rick: So. 19, 190, 6-2
PEORIA (Richwoods)**

Rick made huge strides in spring practice, sewing up the No. 2 split end assignment behind Bruce Hubbard. His performance during the spring established him as the top receiving prospect among the sophomores-to-be. He has excellent moves for working his way into the open, and his better than average speed makes him an open field threat. He's conversant with the throwing end of a pass, too, having played quarterback in high school, where he also lettered in basketball and track.

Saturday, July 31

After practice I like to stick around and work on punting. I didn't punt last year, but I did enough my junior season to last a lifetime. But I know that the more things you can do for the team, the better your chances of making the roster.

I call Kerry Reardon the fastest redhead in the world. We played DBs in the East-West Shrine Game together, and then we both got drafted by the Chiefs. Today he stayed out with me and we punted balls back and forth over Stram's tower. I think Hank might have seen us. I remember in the East-West Game Kerry had one punt that almost went backward. The wind in Oakland was blowing around and swirling like crazy. But it was funny as can be.

Kerry is also the guy who keeps track of people's positions on the team. You can go to his room and talk. When guys get cut, he makes adjustments and he can tell you whether it's looking good or bad. I seem to be safe for now. But I wonder if Kerry really knows anything at all. Who knows anything but Coach Stram?

We're three games into the football season, and Zack's twig-like arms are covered with bruises. There is a scab on his neck. Nicks on his legs. But last week he caught a 65-yard pass and then made receptions on three plays in a row. He nailed a kid on punt coverage. "He's a tough kid," says one of our volunteer dads, Jim Covert, a two-time Pro Bowl lineman for the Bears in the '80s.

Yes, but he's a kid with a high voice, a mere toothpick. I sometimes see him in a chair in his room, drawing skateboards, singing to himself. He has stuffed animals on his bed. I worry.

At NFL Commissioner Paul Tagliabue's press conference at the 2004 Super Bowl in Houston, I see Willie Lanier for the first time since I quit playing. Lanier is there for some kind of NFL alumni award. I know he doesn't remember me—I would have been a short-lived insect in his universe—but he is more than happy to talk about old times.

What I am curious about is what the star middle linebacker learned from football. Discipline, perhaps?

"I didn't learn much about discipline from football," he says. "I had that. I won a trip to Florida at age 14 for delivering newspapers. Daily, without fail."

What he did learn, he says, is that striving for perfection in the game could enable him to transcend the limits placed on him by white society. Indeed, he was the very first successful African-American middle linebacker in the NFL. Teams back then had to be white up the middle—quarterback, center, middle linebacker, free safety—the "thinking" positions. The Chiefs came from an outlaw league, the AFL, and they didn't care. Or not as much. Their biggest enemy was the blue-blooded NFL. Still, a black man better not screw up, especially one like Lanier, from a tiny black school like Morgan State in Baltimore.

"Football allows one to reach further than you can ever imagine," he went on, sounding almost like a preacher in the pulpit. Though he wasn't obese, his neck was so huge it spilled out of his collar like sausage from a wrapper. "My point was to do everything at such a high level that it would undermine anyone who might question me as a black man."

That meant playing virtually mistake-free. In his 11 seasons Lanier estimated he took part in "maybe a thousand plays a year, 11,000 total. And I only had five penalties."

I ask him if he can list them for me, and he does. "In 1968 against the Broncos, I hit the center with 50 seconds left in the game because the man said I had punched him and called me a prima-donna. In 1972 or 1973 against the Baltimore Colts in Kansas City, Marty Domres was running out of bounds, then he cut back and I clotheslined him. I had no choice. There was an offsides against the Steelers in '74— I mistimed a blitz. And in 1975 a San Francisco 49er hit me with an elbow after the play. I started to throw a punch, but I stopped the punch. I said to myself, 'I can't do that.' The official who made the call later reviewed it on film and rescinded it."

And the fifth?

"The fifth one isn't clear. It's always hard. I just can't remember."

I mention to him that for years the Chiefs had more black defensive starters than anybody in the league. He looks at me curiously for a spell.

"There were eight," he says after a time. "And then after Johnny left, there were nine."

That would have been free safety Johnny Robinson.

"I hadn't thought about that," Lanier says. "Hmm. That's interesting."

The press conference was long over and the grand ballroom was almost empty.

"Rick, I'll tell you what I did learn from football. One person can affect the whole. Coaches used to say, 'Because of your race, you have to be better than the best.' A man sees that in football he can improve the lot."

"There was a logical guy to replace John Hostetler at quarterback," says Tom Peeler. "It was———. I guess he had the physical tools, but in the huddle he was a pain in the ass. He built animosity.

"You were a great athlete, but when you were a junior wide receiver, we were playing Manual for homecoming and it was halftime and we're in a classroom and I'm giving my talk. There were Venetian blinds on the windows, and I can see way in the back of the room Telander is pushing the blinds aside and watching the halftime festivities. I wanted to jump you, I was so mad. But when I was done, I yelled at you and said what did I just say? And you repeated everything perfectly, and I just said to the team, 'OK, let's go.'"

Man, I feel terrible. I remember the wandering mind, the fidgety stuff, the rebelliousness, even. But I don't remember that incident. I didn't mean to be disrespectful, I tell him now. I promise.

He smiles, that thin little country smile.

"I'd already seen you in track the previous spring. I was the assistant coach, and we had just won the conference meet, at Pekin. We're sitting in the infield, eating hamburgers, and I look out, and there you were, way off, throwing the shot. And you had never done it before, and you were throwing 46-47 feet. You would have *placed* in the championships. You were flexible and tough, and I knew I could teach you."

And that was enough?

"You were a leader. And you did act the part."

I tell Coach how much the quarterback experience meant to me.

He sighs.

"I didn't always handle it right with other quarterbacks," he says. "Oh dear, I got so arrogant, I thought I could teach anybody anything. One quarterback I yelled at so much. I was on him all the time for everything. And the thing was, he was already good enough. That arrogant bug. I wish he had told me, `You son of a bitch! You can't talk to me that way!'"

How odd. Peeler never yelled at me without cause, never put me down. He gave me the week's play selection on Monday, let me study it, went over the reasons for each formation, each nuance, and then—in perhaps the greatest show of respect and trust I have encountered in my life—let me call every play in every game myself. Dear Lord, the power he handed me, the assurance he gave with a simple nod of the head and then the quiet, plain-as-prairie-grass, "Go get'em, Rick."

There were players, he continues, whom he kicked off the team with a heavy heart. Players like the terrific fullback who was a year ahead of me. A 50-foot shot-putter and sprinter who was tough, weighed 210, had massive thighs, and could hang on the rim.

"You have a responsibility when you play football, to the coaches, to the players, to everyone. He missed practice, and you can't have that. Eleven people and one doesn't do his job, and it all fails. Responsibility.

"In that championship game against Deerfield, their quarterback stumbled and fell on the last play of the game, and that was their last chance to win. Supposedly he just fell. But here's what really happened. Norman Douglas, our defensive right guard, drove their left guard into the backfield enough that his foot was in the quarterback's way. It isn't the quarterback stumbling. It's the quarterback getting tripped. But you couldn't see it at the time. You had to see it later, frame by frame.

"Now, I had cut Norman from the team the year before. He missed a preseason practice with no excuse, and when he showed up for the next one, I just pointed my finger and he knew. Responsibility. That's it. But he came back the next year, and he was dedicated. There's what I call 'football courage.' It's a different thing. Because the game isn't fair to everybody. I made so many mistakes, but think about what Norman Douglas achieved."

I'm still upset about that Bergan game, I tell him.

"I can't believe I ran the wrong way on a bootleg I called myself."

"I've thought about that game quite a bit, too," he replies. "They came out with that lonesome end nonsense, stole it from Army. What difference does it make? That end takes one of your players out of the game. So? I wasn't very smart in that game. I couldn't communicate what I felt."

"Still, I was the one running the wrong way. And I have no idea why."

"My son David was our quarterback, and he ran the wrong way about once a game. Greg was first-team All-State and I remember him taking off the wrong way."

The coach shrugs again. Stuff happens.

It's late and I have a long drive ahead of me. We bid each other farewell. As we shake hands, I wish the clasp would never end

In my car I look back at the house. Responsibility. How many times I've failed.

This photo is the worst.

I have studied the shots that came moments before—me in the East-West Shrine Game tumbling to the cold turf at Oakland Coliseum, waving at the pass from quarterback Dan Pastorini that will soon nestle in wide receiver Mel Gray's outstretched hands for the winning touchdown. Variations of that circus clown's fall made the front pages of the sports sections for the *Oakland Tribune* and the *San Francisco Examiner* the next day. They probably made a lot of other papers, too.

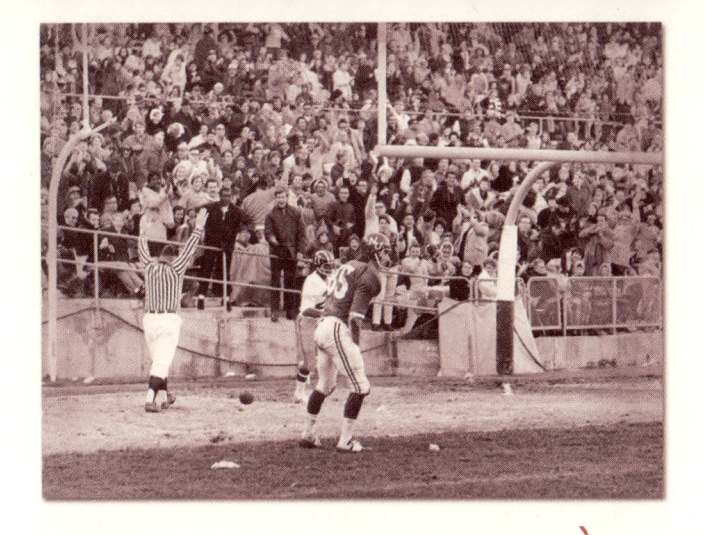

But the enlarged black and white photo I am looking at was taken when the play was over. The referee is signaling a touchdown in front of the cheering end zone crowd, the ball is resting on the painted grass, and wide receiver Mel Gray is starting to trot back toward his celebrating team. And then there is me.

I am hunched pitifully in the foreground, slack-jawed, shell-shocked, my eyes focused on something far, far away. The photo could be labeled Humility and sold as a poster, though Humiliation would probably be more accurate. I do wonder if at least momentarily there can be a worse feeling in sports than that experienced by a defensive back who has given up a long, game-winning touchdown bomb in front of a full stadium and a national TV audience. And this was long. Forty-five yards. In the ensuing years I talked to both Gray and Pastorini, and each admitted that the triumphant TD had helped propel him to his lengthy NFL career. It wasn't a great pass or a great pattern. Both admitted as much. But I slipped and fell, making such matters irrelevant. Slipping, after all, is part of the game. Both players had question marks by their names before that contest, which came a month before the draft. I helped eliminate the question marks.

The miscue—my failure—has stayed with me for a long time. And it hurts every time I think of it.

But as time goes by another feeling has almost transcended the pain. It is this. I am proud that I was there, taking a shot.

Two weeks later I get a letter from Peeler. There are snapshots of the two of us enclosed. "Dear Rick—Hope these photos aren't too late. I really enjoyed our visit. I'm quite proud of the man you have become.

Best, Coach...or Tom (you're old enough to call me that)."

Yes, I'm old enough, Tom.

But Coach will do just fine.

The Scottish romance novelist and poet Sir Walter Scott, the guy who wrote *Ivanhoe* and *Rob Roy*, also wrote a poem called, "Then Strip Lads, and To It." A funny title, I always thought. But his point is, "Get out there, you feisty youngsters, and wallop each other." Best lines:

There are worse things than a tumble on heather,
And life itself is but a game of football.

Of course, what did Sir Walter know? He was born in 1771 and died in 1832. The first documented game of football was played between Princeton and Rutgers in 1869. Guys wore turbans on their heads. But writer Scott knew about tough breaks. He got rich early and then his publishing firm, in which he was a partner, went bankrupt in 1826, and he spent the rest of his days working to pay off his debts.

A tumble on heather would have been far better.

I have railed against the corruption of football, particularly at the college level. But my fight has been against the powers-that-be, the moneyed exploiters—such as television networks which see college football only as entertainment and have now brought "Saturday's game" to us seven days a week—not the sport itself.

Eric Hutchinson was the free safety in our Northwestern secondary. He was good, very good. He was a two-time All-Big Ten selection, and he made some All-America teams the season after I left. He had the uncanny ability to be in places afield he wasn't supposed to be. Many times I would look up to see him coming to my rescue, like the Lone Ranger swooping down on a besieged wagon train.

Hutch, now a teacher/coach and married father of three boys in Ohio, wrote to me in 1990, a long letter touching on the book I had just written criticizing money-driven, big-time college football. He delved into his own reasons for playing the game—purity, desire to achieve, joy—and he ended thus: "From the future unexploited or less exploited, thanks for having the conscience to add a voice of sanity against the overwhelming corruption, when I'm sure it would have been much more comfortable to stay on the sidelines. You get my 'Cool Hand Luke Award.' Remember the scene where the guard is locking Luke into solitary confinement, and he says sheepishly, 'Sorry, Luke, just doing my job'? Cool Hand looks the guard square in the eye and says simply, 'Just doing your job don't make it right.'—Sincerely, Eric"

Football doesn't mean following blindly. It never should mean that.

The reverse has been a long time developing, and Zack is closing fast from his safety position. The other team's flanker, number 32, peels back full tilt, out of Zack's vision, and launches himself into Zack, his helmet under my son's jaw, and both boys are flying through the air, feet off the ground, and I know that Zack is unconscious before he hits the grass. I sprint onto the field, and the trainer is already there, a woman with a blonde ponytail, and she is kneeling beside Zack as he lies flat on his back. His eyes are closed and he is not moving. I look at his little boy's face through his big man's armor, and I feel as though I am looking at all my sins, all my stupidity, all my ignorance.

I hold his limp hand. Finally his left foot is moving. He is moaning. The trainer asks me to hold Zack's helmet steady as she checks his legs, his arm. Earlier in this game Zack had been part of a big pileup on a kickoff, and his lip had been bloodied and he had been slow to get up. The trainer had given him the concussion test. *What grade are you in?* "Sixth," he had replied. "I mean, seventh." School had just started. He laughed. She didn't.

What were the three words I asked you to remember? "Textbook, car, water bottle," he said. He was right. Even I had forgotten them. But there are no concussion tests now. None needed. There is a ragged scrape on Zack's jaw line where the main force of the blow was focused.

My senior year in college I was second-team All-Conference behind Ohio State defensive back Jack Tatum. I watched what Tatum did to wide receiver Darryl Stingley in the NFL, paralyzing him with a head-hunting blow. I still see Stingley occasionally in Chicago, usually at sporting events such as Bulls games. We will shake hands, or rather I will shake his, and we'll chat a bit. And then Stingley will whir off in his wheelchair. *How could I let my son play this game?*

Finally, Zack is alert. Minutes have gone by. He is helped to his feet. He walks to the bench and sits down, and his teammates applaud, as do the few people in the stands. I want to vomit. But I can't.

Sunday, August 1

I've stayed after practice a couple times, doing some punting. I also like to shag balls for Jan Stenerud. He's the Chiefs' soccer-style kicker, and he told me he used to mostly be a skier, which is funny. But then if you think about it, skiers should have strong legs, and Stenerud sure does.

He'll start at the 20-yard line, lazily popping balls through the goal posts, then work back to the 50.

By that time his leg is loose and the ball just roars off his foot. A couple times as I stood at the back of the end zone the ball sailed over my head—long enough, I guess, for 65-yard field goals.

Today when I was walking off the field I found a Jan Stenerud bubblegum card. "Hey Jan!" I yelled. "Look, you're famous! Your handsome face is on this beautiful autographed card!"

He scrutinized the soggy thing for awhile. Then he said, "Aw, it's yust an old picture, anyway." Then he laughed. He's a real nice, modest guy and one of my favorites at camp.

Emily Dickinson is a poet I admire. She seldom left her gardened retreat in Amherst, Massachusets, but in her way, she was tough as nails. She wrote about bees and clouds and daisies, and within her quiet realm she unlocked the universe:

> For each ecstatic instant
> We must an anguish pay
> In keen and quivering ratio
> To the ecstasy.

For every joy, there is suffering. The bigger the thrill, the bigger the hurt.

It is an equation.

Jack Rudnay was a center for the Chiefs. He was a Northwestern alum, two years ahead of me.

I very much appreciated the fact he was looking out for me during those early days. The men I saw daily at camp were the largest men I had seen in my life. One day at lunch mammoth Ed Budde had pointed at my fishnet jersey, so nice and cool these summer days. He grunted, "Give it a rest, kid. Know what I mean?" And I never wore the jersey again.

What Rudnay did that was so very kind was he told the veterans I didn't have to stand on my chair and sing the Northwestern fight song until Mike Adamle joined me in camp from the All-Star game and we could do a duet. Adamle finally showed up, but by then everybody had forgotten.

The reason I was terrified of singing the fight song solo, stupid as it sounds, was because I didn't know the words.

Monday, August 2

Jerrel Wilson is our punter, and he lives right across the hall from me. He's a Texas guy, I think, and he's got a cowboy accent. I amble into his room at various times, to talk about punting and also to see if he can give me any inside information. He seems to know quite a bit about the inner workings of the club.

"Well, Rick," he said one day, "I ain't heard any new news."

I sat in a chair. Jerrel has a really strong leg, like a high-compression spring. Sometimes I wondered what I could do if all I did was focus entirely on one thing, such as punting. But then I didn't even punt once Marty McGann got to Northwestern.

"But I'm happy as a pig in mud," he said. " 'Cause I just signed myself a new five-year, no-cut contract."

"That's tremendous!" I said, thinking how I would feel if anything like that was offered me. As it was, I cringed whenever a coach walked by.

"I'll tell you what I want to do," Jerrel continued. "I want to kick for fifteen more years. And be great, too. The greatest and oldest punter ever to step on a football field."

A little gleam of mischief flashed in his eyes. "Right now I gotta get the fellers together for a friendly game of cards."

I don't know if it was excitement over his newfound luck or sympathy for those less fortunate than he, but between lunch and afternoon practice Jerrel managed to lose more money at poker than anybody I've ever seen.

"I'll get it back," he said still smiling. "Don't worry. It all evens up in the end."

Zack and I have just watched the movie *Jackass* for the second time. The first time was in a theater; this one was from our TV room couch. The documentary film, about a group of young men performing idiotic, dangerous, stunningly juvenile pranks on one another, themselves, and perplexed bystanders is among the stupidest movies ever made. When Zack and I saw it at the theater, I slid off my seat within seconds, overwhelmed with uncontrollable laughter. Afterward we staggered into the lobby and Zack said, "My stomach hurts so much, I might die."

I think you would call *Jackass* a guy movie. How to explain it to a woman? Wife Judy came into the den at random times during our home viewing, watched the video for moments, smiled, frowned, and said in utter disgust, "Zack, you'd better never do that!" and "That is just sick!" and "That is not funny!"

No question about it. She is right on all counts. Still, when Wee-Man kicks himself in the forehead with his boot—on purpose—I almost wet my pants. Again.

And when Zack and I are walking down the sidewalk somewhere, anywhere, we inevitably

Like a Rose 135

will start hitting each other. And before long we're on the ground, wrestling. Or maybe we're locked in a push fight, each grunting sadistically, "Low man wins!"

We truly, truly, truly—truly—can't help it.

Zack is 13, his concussion is long gone, and he is maniacally fired up to play football with the eighth-graders.

I couldn't stop him now without ruining him.

Tuesday, August 3

Before practice I asked Willie Mitchell what he did in the off season.

"Nothing."

"Nothing at all?"

"Nothing."

"You mean you don't work or go anywhere?"

"Nothing."

"Doesn't it get boring after a while," I asked, "just sitting around doing nothing, not even a hobby or anything?"

Uh-uh.

"Man, I don't know if I could stand that. I usually have to be doing something or other."

"Well, you wait till you stop a few end sweeps with two pulling guards an' a 250-pound fullback running like a late train an' then you tell me if in the off season you maybe don't feel like doing too much. You'll probably know what I mean then."

It is Thanksgiving, '03. The two college daughters, Lauren and Cary, are home from school. Robin, the high school daughter, is off somewhere. After the turkey meal and massive dessert Lauren, Cary, Zack and I go to the field behind our house and play tackle football — Lauren and me against Cary and Zack.

The girls are tough, being college swimmers and water polo players. I know I said football is a guys' game, but those two can dish it out. In a powder puff game against another sorority, Lauren broke a defender's nose with a forearm.

Now we sling each other around, and I curse my gimpy knee that lets Cary beat me to fum-

Like a Rose

bles. Lauren and I get walloped by Zack and Cary's passing attack, and we lose big.

It's a cold, soggy day, but the defeat fades fast. Goodness, was that fun.

Wednesday, August 4

After expecting it for days then not believing it could happen then knowing that it was coming yet still hoping for some type of reprieve or some work of Divine Providence, it finally happened—I got the Big Axe.

At breakfast Tom Bettis the D.B. coach called me aside. Oh Christ. A hot flash went through me like a little early morning knife.

"Rick, Coach Stram wants to see you after breakfast."

What for? I pleaded with myself. Oh no, it couldn't be me. But then, why not?

Maybe he just wants to talk.

Well, hell, they just cut Goldie Sellers; that means there is only me and Jim Kearny at strong safety. They couldn't cut me too and leave Kearny by himself. I must have looked puzzled.

"Oh, and Rick," Coach Bettis continued in a voice much too gentle for his personality, "take your playbook with you."

He probably could have heard my heart hit the floor, it fell so fast, so sudden. "Taking your playbook with you" is the official kiss of death at training camps throughout pro football.

Scenes from *Paper Lion* flashed in my mind, and the horrible suspense of waiting to be cut described by George Plimpton took on ironic meaning. I'd laughed when I'd read the book, but then I never expected to be in a pro camp. What did a Sunday quarterback know about the feeling of being dropped from the sport that has been a part of your life for 15 years?

It's over, I kept thinking. That's it. No more worrying about weight, or endurance, or ability to check off red dog blitzes against the triple wing. No sweating out long anguished hours before games, no raw, tender skin continually irritated by ankle tapings. No more touchdowns scored against me.

No more close coverage on a wide receiver who has turned the hundred in 9.4 and knows that in half a football field he can lead me by a step and a half.

No, no more of that. No more of the sick, queasy feeling in my stomach from drinking too much Gatorade too fast after a hot, punishing practice, and no more muscle cramps torturing me late at night as I try unsuccessfully to sleep off the weariness of two-a-days.

In fact, I thought as I headed down the deserted corridor to Coach Stram's office, football has meant little more to me than a succession of pains—a sort of stoic resignation to discipline and hurts of all kinds.

Maybe it is time to get out, I thought. Who needs it, really.

But as I entered the coach'es office I saw the gleaming trophies of past victories—Super Bowl cups, conference trophies, All-Star rings—articles meaningless in themselves yet powerful in their symbolism.

Each trophy signified a dream come true, someone's potential tested to its limit and recorded as a success. The gleaming heap of stainless steel, silver, and jewels lay like a king's treasure, dazzling my eyes, clouding my mind.

And suddenly I wanted just one more chance, one more opportunity regardless of the pain and self-sacrifice to test myself again—one more opportunity to prove myself, to be a success, to do something well.

Through the swirling haze in my mind a song kept reappearing, working its way into my consciousness. It was a sad, bluesy song with a plaintive voice:

In my mind it was sung by an old, old man who once was rich and now has lost everything. He knew life was short, but he had never felt like he did now, which was nothing but lost.

Then I was standing in front of Coach Stram, small, stout, impeccably dressed—a baron in his realm. He was speaking.

"—on waivers for 24 hours. Then if you are not picked up by another team you become a free agent."

Another chance is all I want.

He was smiling kindly, looking directly into my eyes.

I remembered a quote from one of the other coaches in the NFL. "This is a business. We must deal in talent, not personalities."

A hand shook mine forcefully.

"Good luck, Rick."

"Yes, thank you," I said, and I left.

I stopped thinking about significances and future plans and past glories. I walked slowly to my room and began packing the small suitcase I had brought with me.

I really didn't have much to pack, just some dirty clothes and an old pair of football shoes. Then I picked up my battered guitar and finished the melody that was lingering in my mind. The whole dorm was empty so no one could hear, and I was glad for that.

I sang while I strummed the strings, and this was ironic since I had only learned to play the guitar at all during the free time I'd had in football training camps. There were the evenings in the NU dorm with NU quarterback Darryll Splithoff showing me chords on his Country Gentleman, and the times in the frat house stairwell with Doug Macomber, the pole vaulter, teaching me Beatles songs on his accoustic.

I sang pretty quietly now. I sang about going to the airport and getting on a plane, about never passing this way again. My expectations were gone, just like the old man's.

It was over for me.

And that was the sad, unfortunate truth.

I sat for a while, looking at the last page. I re-read it. I flipped back, then forward. Images of myself as a young man hovered in my mind. I could smell the game. I could smell the grass. Hell, I could smell the grass stains. The smell of my helmet. The smell of cut tape. The basement was silent. Every now and then a water pipe would gurgle or a truck would shift gears down the road, but then the silence would return.

It was over. That kind of football was long gone for me. Way long, long gone.

But it was just starting, too.

I thought of all the things football had taught me. There were the obvious things.

Discipline. Even if Willie Lanier already had his. The importance of listening to instructions. Helping somebody simply by doing your job. The awareness that there are no shortcuts to goals. Yeah, I limp because of football. But I also limp because of basketball and games, generally. And if it weren't from football, I would limp because life makes everybody limp.

And there were other lessons, too. Colliding with things is just a whole damn lot of fun. Leaping into the air without concern for your landing is joy. Testing yourself is necessary. Pain does not have to be evil. Football ends. Like everything you care about, like everything you desire. It must. The clock runs out.

And you will lose.

Imagine, Dick Butkus and Gayle Sayers—two of the greatest football players in history—never played in a postseason game. And so you have to accept losing. No, not accept. You process and store and sift losing. You turn it in your hand and look at it from all angles. You see that loss is inevitable and that your thirst can never be quenched and that everything will some day wither away and be gone. And you decide what that means to you.

Football teaches you that life is hard, but it can be immensely rewarding. Even thrilling. Joseph Conrad said we live as we dream, alone. And that is true. But sometimes we come together in teams. Which is another football gift.

The Buddhists have an expression for the inability of people to experience precisely the same thing at the same time, such as a flower. The flower is there, but your perception is different from mine. This is its "unfindability." Said the Dalai Lama, during his famous Central Park speech in New York City: "When we look for the flower among its parts, we are confronted with the absence of such a flower."

But I have my football flower. Its perception changes in my mind, and it shimmers. I hope you have your own flower. If you look at the same flower as I do, we will not see the same thing. And if I look at yours, I will not see what you see. Its petals turn, this one. But it is always there.

And, for me, it is a rose.

THINGS LEARNED FROM FOOTBALL: Out of bounds lines and end zones are a blessing. They don't exist in the real world.

I am on a highway. It is late summer.

Through my windshield I see a crow being chased by a red-winged blackbird. They are framed against the blue sky like letters on a vase.

They fly on.